KENTUCKY FAMILIES

A Bibliographic Listing

by **Donald M. Hehir**

HERITAGE BOOKS, INC.

Other Heritage Books from
Donald M. Hehir:

Georgia Families: A Bibliographic Listing of Books About Georgia Families

Published 1993 by

HERITAGE BOOKS, INC.
1540-E Pointer Ridge Place,
Bowie, Maryland 20716
(301) 390-7709

ISBN 1-55613-869-5

Dedication:

To Donald O. Virdin,
Author, Bibliographer,
and Genealogist, whose
Virginia and Pennsylvania
Genealogies and Family Histories
and personal encouragement gave
rise to my own interest in the field.

ACKNOWLEDGEMENTS

Particular thanks are due to Karen Ackermann at Heritage Books for her very helpful advice on putting this, and other works, together.

TABLE OF CONTENTS

INTRODUCTION

The works in this bibliography (nearly 1500) deal with families who have some connection to Kentucky. By far the largest portion of these works can be found at the Library of Congress in Washington, D.C., the National Genealogical Society (NGS) Library Arlington, Virginia, or in the Daughters of the American Revolution (DAR) Library in Washington, D.C.

Also included are a significant number of books from more than 15 historical association and public libraries from Massachusetts to California, including the New York Public Library, the Allen County Public Library (Fort Wayne, Indiana), and the San Francisco Public Library.

The user should remember that no work of this kind can ever be complete. Many family histories are privately printed and never make their way into large collections. Similarly, many newer works will not have been published, or cataloged, in time for inclusion in this book.

In a work of this kind, it is neither possible, nor practicable, to review individual bibliographies and family histories. For this reason, family names included here may, or may not, be primarily or exclusively associated with Kentucky and some works, published in Kentucky and included here, may occasionally refer to non-Kentucky families . There may be other published material on the same name, or the same family, in other areas of the country. Many of the books cited here included references to other states and countries.

This work follows primarily the Library of Congress system for cataloging names, so, for example, a work on "Cline" might be shown under the Library of Congress Family Name Index of

"Kline" even when "Kline" is not mentioned in the title or the description of the book.

However, since different libraries catalog publications with slightly differing classification systems, family names may have different spellings, depending on the system being used. As a result, there are listings in this book, which may in some cases be duplicative of other listings, since it was not always possible to determine if references were to the same book, to different editions, or to different books.

In compiling the bibliographies and family histories listed, I have attempted to err on the side of including, rather than excluding, works with similar titles and publication dates where the possibility exists that the books are, at least, different editions of the same work. The Cross-Reference Index will show the page location in this book of all families mention in the library descriptions of the source works

Among the various sources, the use of the terms "pages" and "leaves" is not consistent from library to library, so that the same book in different libraries may be shown as having "n" leaves, or "n" pages. Similarly, different catalogers may use different styles to indicate pagination, e. g. 47 pages in one source may appear as 2, 1, 44 pages in a different source, yet both are indicating a total of 47 pages. For this reason it was not always possible to distinguish whether different catalogers were reporting on the same, or different, editions, of the same book. In the interests of simplicity, I have shortened some lengthy pagination descriptions so, for example, a library pagination description of 5p., l., 145, (1)p,, 1 l., is rendered here as 5, 145, 1p.

Where different library catalogers have used different descriptions for the same work, the more detailed description has generally been followed, and in some cases, differing descriptions have been combined to provide the user with as much information possible about the content of an individual work.

FORMAT: The description of bibliographies and family histories contained in this volume generally follows the format indicated below:

FAMILY NAME -- Author (Compiler or Editor). *Title. Subtitle.* Place of Publication, Date of Publication. Number of pages or leaves. Additional Descriptive Material, if any. [Source abbreviation. Library catalog or page number in that source for the referenced work may also be given, e. g. L600 shows that the genealogy is listed as item 600 in Genealogies in the Library of Congress].

ABBREVIATIONS FOR SOURCES

Each source and its abbreviations are given as:

A - Appendices to KAMINKOW, Marion J. Genealogies In The Library of Congress. Baltimore, Maryland, 1972.

C - KAMINKOW, Marion J. Genealogies In The Library of Congress, Second Supplement 1976 - 1986. Baltimore, Maryland, 1987.

D - MICHAELS, Carolyn Leopold and Kathryn S. Scott. DAR Library Catalog, Volume One, Second Revised Edition, Family Histories and Genealogies. Washington, DC, 1983.

DC - GRUNDSET, Eric B. & Bebe METZ. DAR Library Catalog, Volume Three Centennial Supplement: Acquisitions 1985-1991. Washington, DC, 1992.

DS - MICHAELS, Carolyn Leopold and Kathryn S. SCOTT. DAR Library Catalog, Volume One - Supplement - Family Histories and Genealogies. Washington, DC, 1984.

G - GENEALOGIES Cataloged in the Library of Congress Since 1986. Washington, DC, 1992.

L - KAMINKOW, Marion J. Genealogies In The Library of Congress. Baltimore, 1972. 2. v. A-L and M-Z.

NG - National Genealogical Society Library Book List, 5th Edition. Arlington, Virginia, 1988.

NGS - National Genealogical Society Library Book List, 5th Edition Supplement. Arlington, Virginia, 1989.

S - KAMINKOW, Marion J. Genealogies In The Library of Congress Supplement 1972-76. Baltimore, 1976.

VV - VIRDIN, Donald O. Virginia Genealogies and Family Histories. Bowie, Maryland, Heritage Books, Inc., 1990.

VP - VIRDIN, Donald O. Pennsylvania Genealogies and Family Histories. Bowie, Maryland, Heritage Books, Inc., 1992.

X - KAMINKOW, Marion J. A Complement To Genealogies In The Library of Congress. Baltimore, 1981.

XA - Appendix to KAMINKOW, Marion J. A Complement To Genealogies In The Library of Congress. Baltimore, Maryland, 1981.

In the above sources the numbers following the entry in the text refer to the number assigned to the entry in the source publication and not to a page number:

A - C - G - S - D - DC - DS - L

In other sources, the number refers to the page number where the genealogy or family history is located in that source, e. g. NG123 shows that the genealogy is located on page 123 of the National Genealogical Society Library Book List.

NG - NGS

No page numbers are given for X - XA, or VV and VP entries since these sources are not drawn directly from shelf listings or catalogs of libraries.

While most citations are to specific library collections, the Virdin Virginia (VV) and Pennsylvania (VP) genealogies are not contained in any specific library. Library collections for entries followed solely by [VV] or [VP] may be in some of the other library collections cited, but the user is advised to consult other libraries and historical and genealogical societies in the states concerned. All other source references are to libraries and genealogical societies located in the Metropolitan Washington, DC area, except those marked "X-_____ or XA_____".

Note that the entries for the Complement to the Genealogies in the Library of Congress, "X" and "XA", are for genealogies and family histories not in the Library of Congress at the time "A Complement... " was written and many are not in the Library of Congress collection to this date. The coding, at the end of each entry, will indicate if any particular "X" or "XA" entry is also shown as being in the Library of Congress collection. The X is followed, by the initials of the Library, or Libraries, where the genealogy or family history is located, e.g.

[X-FW] Allen County Public Library, Fort Wayne, Indiana

[X-NY/SL] New York Public Library and St. Louis Public Library.

Library Designators used with the "X" (and "XA") entries are:

AH	Alaska Historical Society
BA	Boston Athenaeum
CH	Cincinnati Historical Society
DP	Denver Public Library
FW	Allen County Public Library, Fort Wayne, Indiana
GF	Genealogical Forum of Portland, Oregon
IG	Idaho Historical Genealogical Library, Boise
KY	Kansas State Historical Society, Topeka
LA	Los Angeles Public Library
LI	Long Island Historical Society, Brooklyn, N. Y.
MH	Minnesota Historical Society, St. Paul
NJ	Gloucester County Historical Society, Woodbury, N. J.
NY	New York Public Library
OH	Ohio Historical Society, Columbus
OL	The State Library of Ohio, Columbus
OS	Oregon State Library, Salem
PH	The Historical Society of Pennsylvania, Philadelphia
PP	Library Association of Portland, Oregon

SF San Francisco Public Library

SP Seattle Public Library

SL St. Louis Public Library

SU Sutro Branch of the California State Library, San Francisco

SW Spokane Washington, Public Library

WR Western Reserve Historical Society, Cleveland, Ohio

GLOSSARY

? - Indicates a doubt by the compiler of this work as to the accuracy of the material shown in the original source; Also, indicates a conflict in the data shown in different sources when referring apparently to an identical work.

! - Indicates a doubt by the compiler of the source document as to the accuracy of the material shown in the referenced work.

c. - Circa. (Also, ca.)

ed. - Edition.

enl. - Enlarged,

l. - Leaves.

NAS - No Author or Compiler shown in the source listing.

NP - No Place of Publication indicated.

n.d. - No Date of Publication indicated.

numb. - Numbered.

p. - Page(s).

rep. - Reprint.

rev. - Revised, Revision.

sic _ Used to indicate that the previous word or phrase has been copied precisely from the original source even though apparently misspelled or incorrect.

unp. - Unpaged.

v. - Volume or Volumes.

ABELL -- Abell, William Russell. *Abell, Abel, Able Surnames in the Federal Census of Kentucky, 1800-1850.* Des Moines, IA, W. R. Abell, 1983. iii, 21p. [C1].

ABELL -- Newcomb, Mary. *Brief sketch of the Families of Abell, Craven, Masterson, Miller, Newcomb, Pierceall.* New Hope, KY, 1928. 5p., 25 numb. leaves. [L28].

ACKER -- Acker, Mary T. *Acker Family Trail: Main Acker Family from Caseyville, KY, Evansville, Ind., Nazareth, Texas.* Castro, TX, 1968. 176p. [X-FW].

ADAMS -- Adams, Earl. *The Adams Family History; Descendants of Zadock Adams of Graves County, Kentucky.* Hixson, TN?, Adams, 1985. 170p. [DC12].

ADAMS -- Adams, Katherine K. *Adams Genealogy; Addams -Adams of Maryland...Ganway of Virignia, Concklin of New York, Kellogg of Mass., Williams - Love..., Brownlow of Virginia and Kentucky.* Chicago, IL, Author, 1925. 75 leaves. [X-FW; VV].

ADAMS -- Griffith, Dorothy Amburgey. *Adams families of Southeast Kentucky.* St. Louis, MO, Genealogical Research & Productions, 1986. vi, 190p. 1. Adams family. 2. Kentucky Genealogy. [G3].

ADAMS -- Robinette, E. J. *The Adams Family of Lawrence County, Ky.* ___, KS, E. J. Robinette, 1989. 381, 74p., 5 pages. of plates. 1. Adams family. 2. Kentucky-Genealogy. [G4].

ADAMS -- Wood, Eugene L. *Some Descendents of the Adams, Floyd and Wood Families of Pulaski and Casey Counties of Kentucky and Connecting Families: Anthony, Bailey, Carlisle, Elder, Eubanks, Hoshor, Hubble, Humphrey, McClure, Penick, Wade.* Albuquerque, NM, Wood, 1967. 77, 6, 134 l. [L126; D72].

AHRENS -- Bridwill, Margaret Morris. *The Ahrens Story.* Louisville, KY. 1954. 73p. [L152].

AIKEN -- Wright, Eunice Montgomery. *The Samuel A. Akin Family.* Campbellsville, KY, E. M. Wright, 1977. 57p. 1. Aiken family. 2. Aiken, Samuel A.-Family. 3. Kentucky-Genealogy. [G6].

ALCORNS -- Alcorn, Nellie W. *Eli Greenville Alcorn, 2nd Branch of the Kentucky Alcorns.* Columbus, OH, American Text Book,1958. 44p. [X-FW].

ALLEN -- Allen, Maude Bliss. *Samuel Allin Revolutionary War Soldier, 1756-1841, of North Carolina and Kentucky.* NP, Allen, 1966. 456, 51p. [D175].

ALLEN -- Begley, Jackson Allen. *A History and Genealogical Record of the Allens, Begleys, Mays of Kentucky; the Descendants of John Allen from 1750 to the Present Time.* Cincinnati, OH, Begley, 1949. 137p. [L292; D181].

ALLEN -- Green, Thomas Marshall. *Historic Families of Kentucky with Special Reference to Stock Immediately Derived from the Valley of Virginia; Tracing in Detail the Various Genealogies and Connexions and Illustrating from Historical Sources Their Influence upon Political and Social Developments of Kentucky and the States of the South and West .. 1st Series.* Cincinnati, OH, 1889 or 1890. iv, 304p. [L250; A10].

ALLEN -- Hill, Irene Allen. *The Isaac Allen Family of Tennessee and Kentucky.* Salt Lake City, UT, I. A. Hill, 1990. 258p. 1. Allen family. 2. Allen, Isaac, 1789-1856-Family. 3. Tennessee-Genealogy. 4. Kentucky-Genealogy. [G9].

ALLEN -- Willis, Irene Patterson. *The Descendants of Joseph Allen of Grayson County,*

Kentucky, 1810-1987. Leitchfield, KY, I. Willis, 1987. 103p. 1. Allen family. 2. Fllen, Joseph, 1810-1880-. 3 Kentucky-Genealogy. [G10].

ALLEY -- Allen, Maud B. *Alley - Osbourne Genealogy... of Va., Ky., Tennessee and Indiana.* NP, n.d., (various pagings). [X-LA: VV].

ALLMOND -- NAS. *Lineage of Allen Everard Allmond.* D.A.R. Chart, Louisville, KY. 1960. [L314].

ANDERSON -- Abernathy, Bonita. B. *Whitehaven, Early Years Remembered.* Kevil, KY, B. B. Abernathy, 1983. 55p. 1. Whitehaven (Paducah, Ky.) 2. Anderson, Edward L., 1815-1872- Homes and haunts-Kentucky-Paducah. 3. Paducah-Biography. 4. Anderson-family. 5. Paducah-Buildings, structures, etc. [G12; C14].

ANDERSON -- Anderson, Robert M. *Family Chart of the Andersons of Kentucky & Ohio.* NP, 1902, 1 General Chart. [X-FW].

ANDERSON -- Sanders, Marilyn Miller. *By Watermelon Road to Whipoorwill Creek: A Record of the Family of Thomas Waller Anderson and Mary Frances Hummer of Logan County, Kentucky.* Owensboro, KY, M. M. Sander, 1983. ii, 14p. [C15].

ANDERSON -- Schermerhorn, Sharon Minor. *Supplement to The Tubbs and Quinton Families of Pulaski County, Kentucky: Extending the Line of Pouncy Anderson (b.1794) to His Grandfather David in Louisa Co., Virginia and Tracing the Royal Ancestry of the Quintons to approximately 107 A. D.* Olympia, WA. S. M. Schermerhorn, 1988. 15 l. 1. Tubbs family. 2. Quinton family. 3. Anderson family. 4. Pulaski County (Ky.)-Genealogy. [G13].

APPLEGATE -- Hardeman, Mary Gertrude Nave. *Genealogical Data of the Applegate Family.*

Louisville, KY, Hardeman, 1957. 24 l. [D332].

ARDERY -- Ardery, Julia A. *Ardery (Ardrey) Chart*, Lexington, KY, The Keystone Printery, 1930. Genealogical Tables of the Kentucky, North Carolina, South Carolina, Pennsylvania, and Ohio branches of the Ardery (Ardrey) family. [L503].

ARDER(RE)Y -- Hardin, Bayless. *Chart of Ancestors of William Breckenridge Ardery, (Arderrey) "Roccligan".* Paris, Bourbon County, Kentucky. Frankfurt, KY, 194_. [L504].

ARGALL -- Sharp, John L. *From Adam to the Royalty of England and Scotland, to the Families of Fleming County, Ky.: or the Ascendants of Selvinous Dina Argo.* Moorehead, KY, Sharp, 1976. 56p, 4 l., 48 leaves of plates. [C19].

ARGO -- Sharp, John L. *From Adam to the Royalty of England and Scotland, to the Families of Fleming County, Kentucky.* Morehead, KY, 1976. 56p. [X-FW].

ARNOLD -- Arnold, Edgar F. *The Arnolds of Gwent.* Madisonville, KY, E. F. Arnold, 1985. 58p. 1. Arnold family. 2. Wales Genealogy. [G19].

ARVIN -- Arvin, Martin Joseph. *Arvins Past and Present.* Owensboro, KY, McDowell, 1981. xxi, 94p. [C21].

ATCHINSON -- Barekman, June Beverly. *History of Edmund Etchison, Revolutionary Soldier of NC and His Descendants Including Atchisons, VA, MD, KY, Records of Atchison, Atchinson, Autchersin, Etcheson, Etchison, Ethinson, Eytchison Kin Throughout America.* Chicago, IL, 1980. 264p. [NG16].

ATKINS -- Daniels, Joseph T. *The Adkins Family of Eastern Kentucky and Surrounding*

Areas. Naples, FL, J. T. Daniels, 1988. 238p. 1. Atkins family. 2. Kentucky-Genealogy. [G22].

ATKINSON -- Atkinson, J. B. *Atkinsons of New Jersey from the Records of Friends Meetins and from Offices of Record in the State.* Earlington, KY, Earlington Bee Print, 1890. 40p. [X-FW/LI/MH/PH].

ATWOOD -- Atwood, Raymond Thomas. *Genealogy of the Gilbert Atwood Family.* Hopkinsville, KY, Atwood, 1979. 518, 161p. [C23].

AUBREY -- Aubrey, Walton L. *Aubrey - Awbrey of Virginia and Kentucky.* Lexington, KY, W. L. Aubrey, 1987. 72p. 1. Aubrey family. 2. Virginia-Genealogy. 3. Kentucky-Genealogy. [G23].

AUBREY -- Eldred, Olive (Seaton). *Sketches of the Aubrey Family. Ancestors, and Descendants of John Russell Aubrey and Cornelia Westmore Aubrey, Vandella, IL and Welch, OK.* Paducah, KY, 1973. 98p. [NG17].

AUBREY -- Eldred, Olive Seaton. *Sketches of the Aubrey Family.* Princeton, KY, Eldred, 1973. 4, 98p. [D411].

AUDIN -- Audin, Margaret. *Barking Up That French Tree.* Owensboro, KY, Cook-McDowell Publications, 1980. 61p. [C24].

AUXIER -- Kozee, William Carlos, *Early Families of Eastern and Southeastern Kentucky.* Strasburg, VA, Printed by Shenandoah Publishing House, 1961. 886p. [L650].

B

BACON -- Donaldson, O. Clyde. *Warren Adams Bacon of Bourbon County, Kentucky: His Ancestors and Descendants.* Hopkins, KY, Donaldson, 1989. v, 80p. [DC148].

BAER -- Bare, Eugene and Dora. *Highlights of the Life of Henry Bare Amid the Cliffs of Caney Creek, Kentucky.* Baltimore, MD, Gateway Press, 1984. xxiv, 198p. 28 pages of plates. 1. Baer-Family. 2. Kentucky-Genealogy. [G28; C29].

BAILEY -- Bailey, Alice Morrey. *Callam Holman Bailey, Planter, Early Settler of Barren County, Kentucky.* Glasgow, KY, South Central Kentucky Historical Society, 1983. 173p, 4p. of plates. 1. Bailey family. 2. Kentucky-Genealogy. [G29; C29].

BAIRD -- Huber, Nellie C. & Lewis, Ruth. *The Reverend John Baird Legacy: A Baird History and Genealogy: Level Woods Methodist Church, Larue County, Kentucky, 1796-1986.* Utica, KY, McDowell, 1986. xvi, 216p. 1. Baird family. 2. Baird, John, 1768-1846-Family. 3. Kentucky-Genealogy. [G30; DC157].

BAKER -- Bassett, Miverva Bone. *Some Webster County, Kentucky Families.* Baltimore, MD, Gateway Press, 1983. 193p. [DS29].

BAKER -- Shipp, Ralph D. *A Baker Family Genealogy: Pioneers of North Carolina, Kentucky, Indiana, Missouri, and Iowa and Allied Families, Dunn, Gourley, Russell.* Baltimore, MD, Gateway Press, xiv, 342p, 1 plate leaf. [C31].

BALL -- Hoskins, William W. *John Ball of Lee County, Virginia, and His Descendants; Bell County, Ky., Harland County, Ky.* Radford, VA, Commonwealth Press, 1975. 396p. [X-FW; VV].

BALLARD -- Bridwell, Margaret Morris. *Notes on One of the Early Ballard Families of Kentucky.* Louisville, KY, The Filson Club History Quarterly, 1939. 23p. [D574].

BANTA -- Murray, Joan England. *The Bantas of Pleasant Hill Kentucky: Their Ancestors and Descendants. 1st ed.* Palatine, IL, J. E. Murray, 1985. viii, 120p. 1. Banta family.

2. Pleasant Hill (Ky.)-Genealogy. 3. Shakers -Kentucky-Pleasant Hill-History.
[G33; C35].

BAREKMAN -- Barekman, June B. *Some Bible Records on a Family Named Barackman, Barickman, Barkman, Barrackman, Barrickman, Bergman; from Germany to the Colonies: Va., W. Va., Ind., Penns., Ky., Ill., Md., and Ohio.* Chicago, IL, 1967. 19 l. [X-FW/NY/PH; VV].

BAREKMAN -- Barrickman, June B. & Jones, Hank. *The Genealogy of the Jacob Barrickman Family from Pennsylvania, Kentucky to Franklin, Ripley and Marion Counties, Indiana.* Chicago, IL, 1967. 17 l. [L989; VP].

BAREKMAN -- Barekman, June Beverly. *John Barrickman and His Children of Shelby County, Illinois, Son of Jacob Barrickman, Revolutionary Soldier of Maryland, Pennsylvania, Kentucky, Indiana. Grandson of George Peter Bergmann. Rev. with New Data.* Chicago, IL, Author, 1972. 41 leaves. FW and NY list as BARRICKMAN.
[S138; NG18; X-FW/NY; VP].

BARLOW -- Lindsey, H. B. *Barlow Family of Newport, Ky. (and) Clough Family of Newport, Ky.* Newport, KY, Author, 1928. 6 leaves. [X-FW].

BARNER -- Barner, Konrad von & Ulrich von. *Compilation of History of the Barner Family (Translated From the German by George Brenneaman Barner).* Utica, KY, McDowell Publications, 1980. xii, 318p. [DC193].

BARR -- McCreary, James Bennett. *(Genealogical Chart of the Barr Family.),* Richmond, KY, 1904. [L1071].

BARRACKMAN -- Barekman, June B. *Some Barrackman's (sic) Barrickman's (sic) of La Salle and Livingston Counties of Illinois.* Chicago, IL, Barekman, 1970. 19 l. and rev. ed. 1972. Bound with John Barrickman and His Children of Shelby County, Illinois, a Son of

Jacob Barrickman, Revolutionary Soldier, Lived Maryland, Pennsylvania, Kentucky, Indiana: a Grandson of Georg Peter Bergmann, Born Germany, served in Colonial French Indian Wars in Maryland, and as Patriot in the Revolutionary War in Maryland and Pennsylvania. [D686].

BARRACKMAN -- Barekman, June B. *The Barrackman - Barrickman Families of West Virginia.* Chicago, Barekman, 196-. 76, 25 l. (5 v. bound together). Some Bible Records on a Family Named Barackman, Barekman, Barickman, Barkman, Barrackman, Barrickman, Bergmann, from Indiana, Illinois, Kentucky, Ohio / by June B. Barekman, 1967 -- The Genealogy of Michael Barrickman Family Group of Fredrick (sic) County Maryland and his Sons and Grandsons of Pennsylvania, Ohio, Indiana, Illinois, Iowa, and All Points West and Northwest / by June B. Barekman, 1968 -- An early Barrickman Line in the State of Kentucky / June B. Barrkman, 1969. Barrickman - Barrackman of Crawford County, Pennshlvania / June B. Barekman, 1974. [D688].

BARRACKMAN -- Barekman, June B. Barrackman-Bergmann; *Germany to the Colonies - 1742 through 1961.* Chicago, IL, Barekman, 1962. 2 v. Bound with Bible Records of Barekman, Barkman, Coker, and Hess Families and the Will of Peter Barrickman. [D689].

BARRICKMAN -- Barekman, June B. *An Early Barrickman Line in the State of Kentucky.* Chicago, IL, n.d. 10p., mimeo. [X-FW/PH].

BARRON -- Barron, William P. *The Barron Family of Pulaski County, Kentucky, 1798-1975.* Niles, OH, Family Heritage Publications, 1982. 130p. [C39].

BARROW -- Floyd, William Barrow. *The Barrow Family of Old Louisiana.* Lexington, KY, Floyd, 1963. xviii, 146p. [L1087; D695].

BARTON -- Bowling, Noland. *Meet Your Ancestors: Some Descendants of Edward*

Philpott (1597-1678), William Barton (1605-1674), William Smoote (ca 1597-1673), Moses Hobart (1774-1856). Utica, KY, McDowell Publications, 1985. 398, lxviii p., 1 leaf of plates. 1. Philpot family. 2. Philpot, Edward, 1597-1678 3. Hobart family. 4. Barton family. [G38].

BASHAM -- Basham, Kay Joyce Yates. *The Basham Family History of Breckenridge County, Ky.* Louisville, KY, K. J. Y. Basham, 1984. 1 v. various pagings. [C41].

BASHAM -- Powell, Omegene Powers. *Jerry Basham and Ellen Higgs: Their Descendants and Related Families: Related Families - Aldridge, Bland, Braden, Calloway, Clark, Crask, Harris, Knight, McBride, Neil, Nichols, Powers, Ray, Russell, Salmon, Smiley, Tucker, Wigginton, Wilson.* Utica, KY, McDowell Publications, 1986. 168p. 1. Basham family. 2. Basham, Jeremiah Henderson, 1857-1942-Family. 3. Higgins family. 4. Powell family. [G38].

BASNETT -- Lloyd, Emma Rouse. *The Basnett Family of New Jersey and Kentucky.* NP, n.d. No pages shown. Available for consultation at the Lloyd Library, 309 W. Court Street, Cincinnati, 2?, Ohio. [L1145].

BATCHELDER -- Sterner, Pauline L. *The Ancestry of the Families in Hancock County, Ohio, of Algae, Beck, Schaller, Sterner, and Weitz, and Batcheldor, Clark, Cole, and Lilly in Nelson County, Kentucky.* Findlay, OH, Sterner, 1976. x, 51p. 1. Sterner family. 2. Beck family. 3. Batchelder family. 4. Hancock County-Genealogy. 5. Nelson County-Genealogy. D and FW list under BECK. [G39; D866; X-FW].

BATES -- Halbert, William Carter. *The Bates Family in Kentucky.* New Rochelle, NY, 1955. 3 leaves. [L1177].

BAUGH -- Cott, Nora W. *Bible of Abraham Baugh and Amanda M. Baugh and George Witten*

Faris and Adaliza Faris, Laurel County, Kentucky. Philadelphia, Jesper Harding, 1852. 25 l. [D779].

BAXTER -- Wright, Eunice Montgomery. *The Family of Charles Samuel Baxter, 1838-1922.* Campbellsville, KY, E. M. Wright, 1980. 9 leaves. 1. Baxter family. 2. Baxter, Charles Samuel, 1838-1922. [G41].

BAYLOR -- Baylor, O. W. - Editor. *Baylor's Quarterly v 1. - Official publication of the Baylor Historical Association of America.* Louisville, KY, July, 1930. [L1230].

BEAN -- Bean, Eleanor Elizabeth & Powers, Ralph Monroe. *Bean - Powers Ancestry: Also including Carter, Clark.* Jonesville, KY, Bean, 1985. 2 v. [DC237].

BEAN -- Bean, Richard. *John Bean 1776-1849 of Clark County, Kentucky: His Story and Descendants.* NP, 1979. 119 pages. [DC238].

BEAN -- Beanblossom, Walter S. *Beans of Harrison County, Indiana.* Hawesville, KY, 1973. 40, 3p. [X-FW].

BEARD -- Cowles, Frank. *William Beard of Nelson County, Kentucky and His Descendants.* Baltimore, MD, Gateway Press, Clearwater, FL, 1986. 318, 143p. 1. Beard family. 2. Beard, William, fl. 1763-1807-Family. 3. Kentucky-Genealogy. [G43].

BECK -- NAS. *Some Material on the Beck Genealogy with Special Emphasis on Kentucky and Virginia Lines. Clippings, Written Material and Photographs.* Notebook, Vertical File in the Library of Congress. [L1311].

BECK -- Sterner, Pauline Louisa Beck. [G44]. See above: BATCHELDER. [G39; D866; X-FW]

BECKHAM -- Beckham, James Madison. *Genealogy of the Beckham Family in Virginia and the*

Branches thereof in Kentucky, Tennessee, Pennsylvania and West Virginia with Family Sketches. Richmond, VA, Presses O. E. Flanhart Printing Company, 1910. 80p. [L1318; D870; VV].

BECKNER -- Beckner, William Everett. *The Beckners of Botetourt.* Fort Kansas, KY, 1928. 35 numb. leaves. [L1321].

BECKNER -- Turner, Clara M. *The Beckner Family of Fleming Co., Ky.: with Some Material on Andrew Becker of Grundy Co., Mo.* Beaver Dam, WI, C. M. Turner, 1983. 83 leaves. [C47].

BEDINGER -- Dandridge, Danske. *George Michael Bedinger: A Kentucky pioneer.* Charlottesville, VA, The Michie Company, Printers, 1909. iv, 232p. [L1328].

BEE -- Goode, Cecil E. *Pike County Kin: Accounts of Bryant, Cooke, Bee, and Collins Families of Pike County, Indiana: the Simpson, and Taylor Families of Fayette County, Kentucky: Eaton and Edward Families of Mercer, Washington, and Marion Counties, Kentucky.* Glasgow, KY, C. E. Goode, 1985. ii, 154p. 1. Bryant family. 2. Cook family. 3. Bee family. 4. Pike County (Ind.)-Genealogy. C lists under BRYANT. [G45; C96].

BEGHTOL -- Maes, Virginia Ingles. *The Descendants of Peter Beghtol of Pennsylvania, Kentucky and Illinois by His First Wife Polly Bruner, His Second Wife Catherine Bruner, and His Third Wife Sarah Ann Evans, with Miscellaneous Data on Various Lines of the Beghtol - Bechtol Family and the Evans Family in America.* Redfield, SD, 1942. 4p, 22 numb. leaves. [L1305].

BEGHTOL -- Maes, Virginia Ingles. *The Descendants of Peter Beghtol of Pennsylvania, Kentucky and Illinois by His First Wife Polly Bruner... With Miscellaneous Data on Various Lines of the Beghtol - Bechtol family and the*

Evans Family in America. Rushville, IL, 1945. 4p, 22 numb. leaves. [X-NY; VP; VV].

BELCHER -- Garrett, Hester Elizabeth. *Some Vances and Their Related Families.* Utica KY, McDowell Publications, 1985. 145 p., 14p. of plates. 1. Vance family. Belcher family. 3. Branch family. [G46].

BELKNAP -- Belknap, William Burke. *Memorandum of the Family of Wm. B. Belknap.* Lousville, KY, 1870. Privately Printed for Lafon Allen, and Presented with His Complements to His Kinsmen of the Belknap Line. NP, 1936. 20p. [L1378].

BELL -- NAS. *The Bells of Mason County, Kentucky, Charles Bell and Daniel Bell.* NP. H. Ball, 1981. 1 v. (various pagings). [C50].

BELL -- Bell, Martha A. *Poems of Mrs. Martha A. Bell.* Louisville, KY, n.d. viii, (8)-135p. [L1381].

BELL -- Buland, Geraldine Brown. *Silas Bell of Wayne County, Kentucky, 1787-186_.* Sapulpa, OK, Buland, 1978. xx, 221p., 7 l. of plates. [C50; D924].

BENEDICT -- Pearce, Marvin J. *Benedict Pioneers in Kentucky.* El Cerrito, CA, Pearce, 1968. 73p. [L1434; D942; X-SP].

BENFIELD -- Powell, Omegene Powers. *Frederick Powers and Tresea Powers: Their Descendants, Ancestors, and Related Families.* Utica, KY, McDowell Publications, 1987. 350p., 1 leaf of plates. 1. Powers family. 2. Benfield family. 3. Bolen family. 4. Powers, Frederick, 1814-1890-Family. 5. Kentucky-Genealogy. [G48].

BENNETT -- Kozee, William Carlos. *Early Families of Eastern and Southeastern Kentucky and Their Descendants.* Strasburg, VA, Printed by Shenandoah Pub. House, 1961. 886p. [L1459; VV].

BENNINGTON -- Brumfield, Marcia Conrad. *Thomas Bennington, 1760-1846 and Mary Raines, 1780-1874, (Niece of Simon Kenton).* Mayfield, KY, Brumfield, 1990. 10 l. [DC278].

BENTLEY -- Bentley, William W. *The Bentleys of Eastern Kentucky.* NP, Bentley, 1973. 55 leaves. [S202; D982].

BERNHEIM-- Bernheim, Isaac Wolfe. *The Story of the Bernheim Family.* Louisville, KY, J. P. Morton & Company, Inc., 1910. 5, 145p. [L1519].

BERRY -- Agricola, David V. *The Berry Family of Lawrence Co., Ky. - 1st ed. -* Lakewood, OH, Agricola, 1978. vi, 64p. 1. Berry family. 2. Lawrence County-Genealogy. [G52].

BERRY -- Berry, Michael W. *Records of the Berry Family of Virginia, Kentucky and Georgia.* Washington, DC, Berry, 1987. 166 l. [DC290]

BERRY -- Berry, Russell L. *The Berry Tree in Craven's Country; The James Grimes Berry - Lucinda Craven Family of KY, IL, and MO. including "Westward Wending" by Ray M. Berry.* Brookings, SD, 1986. 48p. [NG21].

BERRY -- Wright, Eunice Montgomery. *Elijah R. Berry, 1838-1869, and His Descendants.* Campbellsville, KY, E. M. Wright, 1985. 20 l. 1. Berry family. 2. Berry, Elijah, 1838-1869-Family. 3. Kentucky-Genealogy. [G53].

BERRY -- Wright, Eunice Montgomery. *Reverend John Berry, 1847-1919, and His Descendants.* Campbellsville, KY, E. M. Wright, 1985. ii, 48p. 1. Berry family. 2. Berry, John, 1847-1919-Family. 3. Kentucky-Genealogy. [G53].

BERRY -- Wright, Eunice Montgomery. *Thomas Berry, Jr., 1851-1939, and His Descendants.* Campbellsville, KY, E. M. Wright, 1985. ii, 68p. 1. Berry family. 2. Berry, Thomas, 1851-1939-Family. 3. Kentucky-Genealogy. [G53].

BERTRAM -- Dalton, Myrtle, B. Ed. *Bertram Book: A Picture Book... and Short Biographical Sketches of about 1300 Members of the Bertram Family in the Vicinity of Sunnybrook, Ky.* Jamestown, TN, 1959. Pages unnumbered. [X-FW].

BEWLEY -- Bewley, Shelby Jackson. *The Bewley Bugle, 1983.* Rineyville, KY, S. J. Bewley, 1983. xv, 187 columns, 26p., 21p. of plates. Includes the Bewleys of Cumberland... by Sir Edmund Thomas Bewley, Dublin, 1902. 1. Bewley family. 2. Ireland-Genealogy. [G54].

BEWLEY -- Bewley, Shelby Jackson. *Bewley Roots in Tennessee.* Rineyville, KY, S. J. Bewley, 1985 -. v. <1 > Anthony Bewley. [C59].

BEWLEY -- Boyd, Frankie Jewell. *Christopher Bewley and His Descendants, 1775-1982.* Utick, KY, McDowell Publications, 1983. viii, 511p. [C59].

BEWLEY -- Cox, Opal London. *Kinfolk.* Enid, OK, O. L. Cox, 1985. v, 390p., 1 leaf of plates. Spine title: Kinfolk: Bedford County, Virginia to Breckenridge County, Kentucky. 1. Bewely family. 2. Dowell family. 3. Yates family. [G54].

BEWLEY -- Debrett. *Research into the Ancestry of William Bewley of McClean County, Kentucky.* Rineyville, KY, S. J. Bewley, 1980. 7, 26 leaves. [C60].

BEWLEY -- Debrett. *Collected Works: Bewley Roots in Virginia and Kentucky.* Rineyville, KY, S. J. Bewley, 1980. v 1. Research into the ancestry of William Bewley of McClean County, Kentucky. [C60; VV].

BEWLEY -- Parker, Donald Dean. *The Bewley and Related Families.* Owensboro, KY, Cook-McDowell Publications, 1980. 130, 5p. 11 leaves of plates. Reprint. Originally Published: Brookings, SD, D. D. Parker, 1946. [C59].

BINGHAM -- Bingham, Sallie. *Passion and Prejudice: A Family Memoir - 1st ed. -* New York, NY, Knopf, 1989. 525p. 1. Bingham, Sallie-Family. 2. Bingham family. 3. Louisville (Ky.)-Biography. 4. Upper classes-Kentucky-Louisville-Biography. [G56].

BINGHAM -- Brenner, Marie. *House of Dreams: The Bingham Family of Louisville. - 1st ed. -* New York, NY, Random House, 1988. 452p., 16p. of plates. 1. Bingham family. 2. Louisville (Ky.)-Biography. 3. Upper classes-Kentucky-Louisville. [G57].

BINGHAM -- Chandler, Daniel Leon & Mary Voelz. *The Binghams of Louisville: The Dark History Behind One of America's Great Fortunes.* New York, NY, Crown, 1897. xii, 292p., 4 p. of plates. 1. Bingham family. 2. Louisville (Ky.)-Biography. [G57; DC312].

BINGHAM -- Tifft, Susan E. *The Patriarch: The Rise and Fall of the Bingham Dynasty.* New York, NY, Summit Books, 1991. 574p., 16p. of plates. 1. Bingham family. 2. Bingham, Barry, 1906-1988-Family. 3.Publishers and publishing -Kentucky-Biography. 4. Educators-North Carolina-Biography. 5. Kentucky-Genealogy. 6. North Carolina-Genealogy. [G57].

BINKLEY -- Doss, Brenda Collier. *Jacob Henderson & Julia (Cagle) Binkley and Their Descendants: a Jacques Timothe' Boucher Sieur De Montbrun Connection. Lim. ed.* Utica, KY, McDowell, 1985. 244p. 1. Binkley family. 2. Binkley, Jacob Henderson, ca. 1820- ca. 1880. [G57].

BLACK -- Black, Howard C. *William Black and His Descendants...of Augusta County, Va., and Clark County, Kentucky.* Cincinnati, OH, 1973. iii, 143p. [X-FW; VV].

BLADES -- Blaydes, Mary Douglas Meriwether. *Mort Than Skin Deep, or, Spotsylvania Ascendants of Maxey Lee Blaydes and Some of Their Connections.* Lexington, KY, Blaydes, 1979. 10, 492p. [C65].

BLAIR -- Blair, John I. *Of Blairs of Kentucky.* Tulsa, OK, 1975. 49, viii p. [X-FW].

BLOYD -- Nichols, Edna Bloyd. *William Bloyd - Bloyed of Maryland, Virginia, North Carolina and Green County, Kentucky and His Descendants.* Baltimore, Gateway Press, 1980. xiii, 333p. [C68; DC347; VV].

BLUE -- Arnold, Jane D. *James Samuel Blue of Union County, Kentucky.* Franklin, KY, 1974. 100p. Also Willis G. Hughes Family. [X-DP].

BLUE -- Blu, Elmer F. *The Descendants of John Blue of Lancaster Co., Pa., South Carolina, Fleming Co., Kentucky, Ohio, Illinois and Indiana.* NP, 1944. 20, 2 l. [D1230].

BOAZ -- Boaz, T. D. *Thomas Boaz (1817-1897) and His Descendants.* McLean, VA, T. D. Boaz, 1989. iv, 619p. 1. Boaz family. 2. Boaz, Thomas, 1817-1897-Family. 3. Indiana-Genealogy. 4. Kentucky-Genealogy. [G64].

BOEDECKER -- Cain, Marilyn Wright Duffner *Wright - Boedecker - Duffner Family Histories.* Oklahoma City, OK, M. W. D. Cain, <1989-1990 > v. <1-3 > Contents: v. 1. Wright family of Virginia, Kentucky & Missouri... v. 2. Boedecker family of Prussia and America... v. 3. Duffner family of Germay and America. 1. Wright family. 2. Boedecker family. 3. Duffner family. 4. Prussia (Germany)-Genealogy. 5. Germany-Genealogy. [G64].

BOGGS -- Cox, Bruce K. *Cox and Kin of Southwestern Virginia and Eastern Kentucky: Including Cox, White, Mauk, Reynolds, Wade, Reed, Dickerson, Boggs, Mabry, Lester, Blubaugh, Jones, Hylton, Skaggs, Cosby, Garland, Fraley, Stegall, Trout, DeHart, and Related Families.* Wakefield, MI, B. K. Cox, 1986. vi, 189p., 2 folded leaves of plates. 1. Cox family. 2. Boggs family. 3. White family. [G65].

BOLEN -- Powell, Omegene Powers. [G65]. See above: BENFIELD. [G48].

BONDURANT -- Riley, Jean M. Hinkle. *The Bondurant Family Genealogy and Family-Lore.* Paducah, KY, J. M. H. Riley, 1988. 97, A-L p., 27 l. of plates. [G67].

BOOKER -- Booker, Charles Lee. *The Bucher / Booker Family, 1686-1990: from Klein Gartach, Wurttemberg, Germany to Frederick County, Virginia to Harrison and Jefferson Counties, Kentucky to Knox and Sullivan Counties, Indiana to the Illinois Counties of Jasper, Macon, Moultrie, Piatt, and Sangamon.* Severn, MD, C. L. Booker, 1990. xvii, 828p. [G69].

BOONE -- NAS. *(The) Genealogy of Daniel Boone.* Hackensack, NJ, 1917. Being Genealogy, a monthly magazine of American ancestry, v. 7, No. 8, whole number 100, p. 113-128. Cover Title: Boone Family Records. [X-CH/FW].

BOONE -- Boone, Jackie Ned. *Descendants of Jesse Boone: Tribe of Israel Boone.* Louisville, KY, W. Boone, 1986. vi, 195, 24, 194p. 1. Boone family. 2. Boone, Israel, 1726-1756-Family. [G69].

BOONE -- Boone, Edward D. *Genealogy of the Boone Family of Maryland.* Baltimore, MD, 1938, 142p. [X-FW].

BOONE -- Ford, Helen Mar. *Boonedale Stories.* Montgomery, AL, Auburn University Montgomery Library Resource Center, 1987. 78, 2p. 1. Versailles Region (Ky.)-Biography. 2. Lexington (Ky.)-Biography. 3. Boone family. 4. Ford, Helen Mar-Childhood and Youth. [G69].

BOONE -- Bryan, Dr. J. D. *The Boone-Bryan History, by Dr. J. D. Bryan a Great Grand Nephew of Daniel Boone.* Frankfurt, KY, The Kentucky State Historical Society, Coyle Press, 1913. 24p. [L1889; NG22].

BOONE -- Bryan, J. D. *The Boone - Bryan History*. Frankfurt, KY, The Kentucky State Historical Society, 1939. 24p. [D1321].

BOONE -- Cooper, J. R. *A Daniel Boone Series, A New Boone Series; A Copy of 25 Articles Pub. in the Lexington Herald (Lexington, Kentucky) 1924, 1925, 1927.* Afton, MO, Mrs. George Giulvezan, 1958. 57 leaves. [X-NY/SP].

BOONE -- Crisman, Leo T. *The Boone Family and Kentucky Baptists*. Louisville, KY, Baptist Historical Society, 1946. 31p. [DC375; X-MH].

BOONE -- Douglass, William Boone. *Outline of the Life and Ancestory of Daniel Boone.* Washington, DC, 1925. 4p. [L1892].

BOONE -- Douglass, William Boone. *...Lineage book; Lineages no. 1.* Washington, American Order of Pioneers, Inc. and Boone Family Association, Inc., NP, 1942. v 1, nos. 1 & 2. No. 1. American Pioneer Records; No. 2. American Order of Pioneers... [L1894].

BOONE -- Mayfield, Reuben N. *... Boone Notes: Family Records of Somes of the Ancestors, Descendants, and Kindred of Col. Daniel Boone*. Johnson City, TN, 1931-33. 27 leaves. [X-NY].

BOONE -- Mayfield, R. N. *Boone Family History,* Johnson City, TN, 1945. 66, 6 l. [X-SL].

BOONE -- Mayfield, Reuben N. *The New Boone History*. NP, n.d., 1 leaf. [X-PH].

BOONE -- Spraker, Hazel Atterbury. *The Boone Family; a Genealogical History of the Descendants of George and Mary Boone Who Came to America in 1717; Containing Many Unpublished Bits of Kentucky History, also a Biographical Sketch of Daniel Boone, the Pioneer, by One of His Descendants*. Rutland,

VT, The Tuttle Company, 1922. 691, (7)p. Allied Families: Bryan, Callaway, Davis-Watts, Douglas, Edwards, Foulke-Hughes, Gentry, Grubbs, Harris, Lincoln, Linville, Mayberry, Morgan, Scholl, Spurgeon, Stoner, Tallman, VanBibber and VanCleve. [L1891].

BOONE -- Spraker, Hazel Atterbury. *The Boone Family*. Baltimore, MD, Genealogical Pub. Co., 1974. 707p. Reprint of the 1922 edition. [X-DP].

BOONE -- Van Hoose, John See. *Van Hoose and Gullet Descendants and Ancestors: Holland, England, and America, 1480-1900 and Allied Eastern Kentucky Families-Boone, Bowen, Bryan, Cantrell, Hill, Keese, McKenzie, O'Bryan, Pelphrey, Pratt, Quillin, Salyer, Webb, Williams*. Cullman, AL, Gregath Co., 1990. 365p. 1. Van Hoose family. 2. Gullett family. 3. Boone family. 4. Bowen family. 5. Kentucky-Genealogy. [G69].

BOSWELL -- Hasskarl, Eula Richardson. *The Boswells of Shelby County, Kentucky*. Ada, OK, E. R. Hasskarl, 1970. v, various pagings. [A69; D1366].

BOSWELL -- Hasskarl, Eula Richardson. *The Boswells of Shelby County, Kentucky*. Ada, OK, 1970, 1978. 2 v. [DC382].

BOTTOM -- Bailey, Jack Dalton. *A History of the Ancestors of Robert Charlie Bottom and Flora Allen Bruner and Their Descendants*. Harrodsburg, KY, J. D. Bailey, 1980. 321p. DC gives 340p. [C77; DC384].

BOTTS -- Williamson, Mamie. *Botts Family Data*. Copied by William and Anne Fitzgerald. Florence, KY, 1954. 10 leaves. [L1968].

BOURN -- Stone, May. *Bourne Family and Connecting Lines of Virginia and Kentucky, 1607-1943*. Kansas City, MO, 1947. Pages unnumbered. [X-FW; VV].

BOURNE -- Katz, Gertrude M. P. *Old Letters, Old Biographies, and Old Family Trees of the Bourne, Morton and Allied Families of Virginia, Kentucky, and Other States.* Valley Stream, NY, 1973-4. 1 vol. unpaged. [X-FW; VV].

BOWEN -- Van Hoose, John See. [G77]. See above: BOONE. [G69].

BOWLING -- Bowling, Katherine L. *Bowling: Thomas Bowling, His Forefathers of Maryland, His Descendants of Nelson County, Kentucky.* NP, K. L. Bowling, 1976. 231 leaves. [DC400]

BOWMAN -- Wayland, John W. *The Bowmans a Pioneering Family in Virginia, Kentucky and the Northwest Territory.* Staunton, VA, The McClure Company, Inc., 1943. 185p. [D1421].

BOYLE -- Boyle, John. *Boyle Genealogy. John Boyle of Virginia and Kentucky. Notes on Lines of Descent with Some Collateral References.* St. Louis, MO. Perrin & Smith Printing Co., 1909. iv, 174p. [L2089; NG24].

BOZARTH -- Carby, Lorenza Duncan. *The Jonathan Bozarth Family.* Clarkson, KY, L. D. Carby, 1985. 3 v. (398 l.) 1. Bozarth family. 2. Bozarth, Jonathan, 1754-1830-Family. 3. Kentucky-Genealogy. [G80].

BRADLEY -- Bradley, Myron. *Eber Bradley (1761-1841) and Some Relations.* Wickliffe, KY, Advance-Yeoman, 1977. 82p. One hundred fifty copies printed. [C82].

BRADLEY -- Quillen, Bess Bradley. *The Generations of Stephen Bradley and Polly Fillinger Bradley.* Ashland, KY, 1973. 80p. [S299; NG24].

BRADLEY -- Stubbs, Francis L. *Daniel and Susannah Bradley of Kentucky and Some of Their Descendants.* Columbia, MO, F. L. Stubbs, 1990. vii, 408p. 1. Bradley family. 2.

Bradley, Daniel, ca.1750-ca.1801. 3. Kentucky- Genealogy. [G82].

BRADSHAW -- Bolin, C. B. *My Bradshaws and Their Allied Families.* Russell Springs, KY, Time Journal Pub., 196_. 134p. [X-FW].

BRANCH -- Garrett, Hester Elizabeth. [G83]. See above: BELCHER. [G46].

BRANSFORD -- Shiver, John A. *Bransford Family History.* Hartford, KY, McDowell Publications, 1978, 1981. 2 v. [D1531].

BRANSFORD -- Shiver, John Arden. *Bransford Family History.* Hartford, KY, 1978. Pages not given. [NG23].

BRANSON -- Branson, George. *Genealogy of the Branson Families in America....* Madisonville, KY, Commercial Printers, 1936. 19p. [X-PH].

BRASHEAR -- Back, Troy L. & Brashear, Leon. *The Brashear Story: A Family History [1637-1963].* Viper, KY, Graphic Arts Press, 1980, 1963. vi, 377p. [DC440].

BRECKENRIDGE -- Breckenridge, Helen. *Descendants of John and Mary Cabell Breckenridge.* Lexington, KY, 1980. 16 l. [NG24].

BRECKENRIDGE -- Dicken Garcia, Hazel. *To Western Woods: The Breckenridge Family Moves to Kentucky in 1793.* Rutherford, NJ, Fairleigh Dickinson University Press, London, Cranbury, NJ, Associated University Presses, 1991. 250p. 1. Kentucky-History-To 1792-Biography. 2. Kentucky-History-1792-1865-Biography. 3. Breckenridge family. 4. Breckenridge, John, 1760-1806. [G85].

BRECKENRIDGE -- Klotter, James C. *The Breckenridges of Kentucky, 1760-1981.* Lexington, KY, University Press of Kentucky, 1986. xviii, 393p. 1. Breckenridge family. 2. Kentucky-Biography. [G85; C84].

BREWER -- Bowman, James F. *The Ambrose Brewer Family, 1753-1855.* Pineville or Barbourville, KY, Sun Pub. Co., 1962. vi, 24p. [D1562; X-FW/NY].

BREWER -- Jones, Roselyne Watts. *The Brewer Family: Ancestors and Descendants of Barney Verbryck Brewer and His Son John Wesley Brewer, Also Maternal and Allied Lines.* Harrodsburg, KY, R. W. Jones, 1982. xv, 405, 105 leaves. 1. Brewer family. 2. Brewer, Barney Verbryck, 1808-1895-Family. 3. Brewer, John Wesley, 1839-1896-Family. [G87].

BREWER -- Souder, Marjorie Ann Morton. *Ancestors of Justice and Alabama Hensley Brewer of Clay County, Kentucky.* NP, 1986. 52 l. [DC450].

BRIDGES -- NAS. *History and Genealogy of James and Molly (S.) Thomas and Drewry and Charity (Calhoon) Bridges.* Uniontown, KY, The Author, 1965. 438p. [X-FW].

BRIGHT -- Ford Georgie Hopkins. *Kentucky Brights and Their Kin, Including the Crabb, Drane, Ford, Hopkins, and King Families.* Berkley, CA, 1929. 168, 30p. [L2287].

BRIGHT -- Mills, Harry Willard. *Descendants of Henry Bright, Senior, (born 1760) of Lincoln County, Kentucky.* Washington, DC, Mills, 1941. 71 l. D gives 69 l. 'Notes on the Culbertson Connection by Ben F. Dixon': leaves 32-40. [L2288; D1605].

BRITT -- Britt, Daniel S. *Genealogy of the Trout, Britt, and Related Families.* Utica, KY, McDowell Publications, 1985. iii, 146p. 1. Trout family. 2. Britt family. 3. Plummer family. 4. Kentucky-Genealogy. 5. Virginia-Genealogy. C lists under TROUT and omits Britt from Title. [G89; C170].

BROMWELL -- Bromwell, Henrietta E. *The Bromwell Genealogy, Including Descedants of William Bromwell and Beulah Hall, with Data*

Relating to Others of the Bromwell Name in America, Also Genealogical Records of Branches of the Allied Families of Holmes... Payne... Rice and Leffler... With Some Descendants of Major Conrad Leffler of Pennsylvania, and of the Rev. Peter Fullenwider, Rev. Jasper Simler, and Jonathan Boone of Kentucky... Denver, CO, 1910. Eighty illustrations from various sources. [VP].

BROWN -- NAS. *Three Kentucky Pioneers: James, William, and Patrick Brown.* Louisville, KY, J. P. Morton, 1930. 22p. Reprinted from Filson Club History Quarterly, v. 4., 1930. [X-FW].

BROWN -- Bardin, B. E. *Dr. Preston W. Brown, 1775-1826...* Frankfurt, KY, Liberty Hall, inc., 1945. 28p. Reprint from Filson Club History Quarterly, Jan. 1945. [X-FW].

BROWN -- Colby, Ruth Brown. *Brown Family, 1848-1977.* Hartford, KY, McDowell Publs., 1977. iii, 53 p., 6 l. of plates. [C91].

BROWN -- Hagwood, Louise Thornberry. *Thornberry, Brown, Herndon, Muse, Loy (Lloyd), Massey (Massie), and Jackson Families.* Clarksville, MS, L. T. Hagwood, Louisville, KY, E. Atherton, 1990. 1 v. (unpaged). 1. Thornberry family. 2. Brown family. 3. Herdon family. 4. Muse family. [G100].

BROWNE -- Stewart, Dorathy Browne. *Once Upon A Time.* Owensboro, KY, Cook & McDowell, 1980. iii, 360p. 19 leaves of plates. C lists under BROWN. [C92; D1742].

BRUNER -- Bruner, Harlan Keith and Henry Albert Bruner. *Descendants of George Peter Bruner: s. of George Michael, s. of Jacob, s. of Joseph Bruner.* Hawesville, KY, Henry Bruner, 1981. 1 v. various pagings. [C95].

BRYAN -- NAS. *Bryan Family of Fayette County, Kentucky; A Series of Ten Articles Pub. in Lexington Herald... Feb 27, 1927...*

Fort Wayne, IN, Indand Public Library, 1966. 134p. [X-FW].

BRYAN -- Cooper, J. R. *Bryan Family of Fayette County, Kentucky.* St. Louis, MO, A. T. Davis, 1856. 97 leaves. (Published in Lexington Herald... 1927). [X-SP].

BRYAN -- Cooper, J. R. *Bryan Family Fayette County, Kentucky.* NP, 1962. 85, 62 leaves. Bound with exercepts from the Draper Collection: Bryan notes to Lyman Draper, collected by Lindsey M. Brien. [D1784].

BRYANT -- Goode, Cecil E. [G103]. See above: BEE. [G45; C96].

BRYANT -- Lane, Annabel W. *History of the Bryant Family of Virginia, Kentucky and Missouri.* Littleton, CO, 1966. [VV].

BUCHER -- Booker, Charles Lee. [G104]. See above. BOOKER. [G69].

BUCK -- Buck, Katherine Raines. *Johnathen Buck and Zuriah Covalt, 1755-1985: A History of Jonathan and Zuriah Covalt Buck's Descendants and Allied Families.* Alpha, KY, K. R. buck, 1985. 165p., 1 leaf of plates. 1. Buck family. 2. Buck, Jonathan, 1755-1831-Family. [G104].

BUCKLER -- Buckler, William Harold. *Buckleriana: Notices of the Family of Buckler: Including a Reprint of Bucleriana (London, 1886) by Charles Alban Buckler, Surrey Herald Extraordinary, 1880.* Baltimore, MD, Gateway Press, Peweel Valley KY, W. H. Buckler, 1988. 390p. Limited edition. 500 copies. 1. Buckler family. 2. Great Britain-Genealogy. [G104].

BULLITT -- Jennings, Kathleen. *Louisville's First Families; A Series of Genealogical Sketches with Drawings by Eugenia Johnson.* Louisville, KY, The Standard Printing Co., 1920. 176p. Contain the Bullitt, Prather,

Clark, Churchill, Pope, Speed, Joyce, Veech, Thurston, Taylor, Bate, and Floyd families. [L2636] .

BULLOCK -- Aker, Mary Bullock. *Bullocks of Virginia and Kentucky and Their Descendants.* Parkville, MO, Aker, 1952. 32, 5 leaves. FW shows 32, 10 leaves. [D1850; X-FW/LA; VV].

BURNETT -- Corkill, Eldon. *Cain-Burnett Kin: Descendants of Bailey Cain (1767/70-1807) of Virginia and Kentucky, and of James Burnett, Who Died in 1797, Pittsylvania County, Virginia.* Dallas, TX, E. Corkill, 1988. 194p., 1 l. of plates. 1. Cain family. 2. Burnett family. 3. Cain, Bailey, ca.1767-1807,-Family. 4. Burnett, James, d. 1797-Family. 5. Virginia-Genealogy. 6. Kentucky-Genealogy. [G108].

BURTON -- Burton, Georgie H. B. *Ancestry of Georgie H. B. Burton... of Lexington, Ky.* Lexington, KY, 1935. 182p. [X-FW].

BURTON -- Harrison, Francis Burton. *Burton Chronicles of Colonial Virginia: Being Excerpts from the Existing Records, Particularly Relating to the Burtons of the Valley of the James and Appomatox; with Especial References to the Ancestry of Jesse Burton of Lynchburg, (1750-1795).* Hartford, KY, Cook & McDowell Pub., 1979. iii, 449p. [C103; VV].

BUSEY -- Franklin, John O. *John Busey Family of Anderson County, Ky.* Lawrenceburg, KY, 1943-4. Various pagings. [X-FW].

BUTLER -- Sue, Jacqueline Annette. *Black Seeds in the Blue Grass.* Carte Madera, CA, Khedcanron Press, 1983. 166p. 1 folder leaf of plates. [C105].

BUTTON -- Button, William Garland. *A Part of the Button Family of Virginia and Its Westward Migration to Kentucky, Texas, Oklahoma, and California from 1666 to 1959.* Waco, TX, 1959. [VV].

C

CAIN -- Corkill, Eldon. [G114]. See above: BURNETT. [G108].

CALDWELL -- Caldwell, Charles Wickliffe. *A Chart of the Known Descendants of John Caldwell.* Danville, KY, 1957. [L2871].

CALDWELL -- Young, James, Jr. *Volume Two of the Kennedy - Caldwell Family Descendants; The Caldwell - Reed Family (1800-1958) or the Descendants of Jane Caldwell (1800-1863) & Josiah Reed (xx-18xx) of Bath County, Kentucky and Sangmon and Menard Counties, Illinois.* NP, 1958. 1 v. (various pagings). [D2051].

CALHOUN -- Calhoun, Logan E. *Calhoon, Calhoun, and Others: the Story of James Calhoon (Ireland) and Eleanor West (Virginia), Their Descendants and the Allied Families of Roberts, West, and Sweat (sic) - 1st ed.* Utica, KY, McDowell Publications, Louisville, KY, 1987. viii, 300p. 1. Calhoun family. 2. Calhoon, James, ca. 1750-1830-Family. 3. West family. 4. Roberts family. 5. Sweet family. [G115].

CALLAWAY -- Bate, Dr. R. Alexander. *Colonel Callaways Preparedness. The Career of Colonel Samuel Henderson, and "Robert Wright Bingham", a Memorial Address by Archibald Henderson. The Transylvania Room by Susan Starting Towles.* Henderson, KY, The Society of Transylvanians, 1941. 2, 42, 3p. [L2889].

CALLAWAY -- Hart, Mrs. A. E. *The Callaway Family of Virginia and Some Kentucky Descendants.* Los Angeles, CA, Hart, 1928. 281 leaves. [D2065; VV].

CALLAWAY -- Hart, Mrs. A. E. *The Callaway Family of Virginia and Some Kentucky Descendants.* Los Angeles, CA, Hart, 1929. 5p, 8-367 numb. leaves. [L2888; VV].

CALLAWAY -- Hart, Jessie W. *Richard Callaway Family of Va. and Ky.* Los Angeles, CA, 1933. 619p. [X-FW; VV].

CALLAWAY -- Sheriff, Pauline Callaway. *Samuel Callaway, His Ancestors and Descendants of Kentucky, Missouri and Elsewhere.* Hollis, OK, Sheriff, 1987. 135p. 1. Callaway family. 2. Callaway, Samuel, 1752 or 3-1822-Family. 3. Kentucky-Genealogy. 4. Missouri-Genealogy. [G115; DC578].

CANBY -- Knox, Joan Ritchey. *A Noble / Canby Genealogy: George Thomas and Louisa (Canby) Noble and Some of Their Relatives, Sedwick, Clare, Wade, Taylor, Hough, Pierpont, 1689-1985.* Richmond, IN, J. R. Knox, 1985. viii, 128p. 1. Noble family. 2. Noble, George Thomas, 1801-1853-Family. 3. Canby family. 4. Sedgwick. 5. Indiana-Genealogy. 6. Kentucky-Genealogy. [G118].

CAMPBELL -- Petty, Gerald M. *Notes on Some Descendants of Duncan Campbell of Ireland and Some Descendants of John S. Darby of Kentucky.* Ann Arbor, MI, University Microfilms, Columbus, OH, Author, 1966. 612 leaves. [D2107; X-CH].

CANNON -- Cannon, Harold and Ellen (Andler) Cannon. *The Descendants of Newton and Betsey (Juett) Cannon of Scott County, Kentucky.* Skokie, IL, Cannon, 1979. 216p. [C112].

CAPERTON -- NAS. *The Killing of Colonel Adam Caperton by Indians at 'Estill's Defeat' near Mt. Starling, Kentucky, March 23, 1782.* Sketch of the Caperton Family, Will of Hugh Caperton of 'Elmwood', Genealogy of Hugh Caperton of 'Elmwood'. Published September, 1918 for Mr. John Hope Caperton and Willaim Alexander Gordon, jr. Louisville, KY, Press of J. P. Morton & Company, 1918. 2p. 3-61p. [L2994].

CARPENTER -- Lloyd, Emma Rouse. *Carpenter Family of Kentucky.* NP, n.d. Pages not shown.(Available for Consultation at the Lloyd Library 309 West Court Street, Cincinnati, 2?, Ohio). [L3028].

CARSON -- Kirkwood, Alberta C. *They Came to Kentucky: Chiefly Relating to Boone, Pulaski, Lincoln, Gallatin and Casey Counties, Ky.* Baltimore, MD, Gateway Press, 1976. xv, 748p. [X-FW].

CARTER -- Jones, Miheepa Harb. *Abraham Carter, Descendants, 1760-1982.* Lexington, KY, M. H. Jones, 1986. 209p. [DC629].

CASSIDY -- Cassidy, Samuel M. *Cassidy Family and Related Lines.* Lexington, KY, S. M. Cassidy, 1985. 664p. 1. Cassidy family. 2. Kentucky-Genealogy. [G127].

CASSIDY -- Cassidy, Samuel M. *Michael Cassidy, Frontiersman - 2nd ed.* - Lexington, KY, S. M. Cassidy, 1985. 83p. 1. Cassidy, Michael, 1755-1829. 2. Pioneers-Kentucky-Biography. 3. Cassidy family. 4. Kentucky-Genealogy. [G127].

CATHEY -- Kraft, Myrtrice A. (C.). *Cathey Cousins.* Covington, KY, 1968. 91, 22p. [X-FW/LA].

CHANCE -- Chance, Hilda. *Chance of Ohio, Virginia, North Carolina, Georgia, Texas, Tennessee, Kentucky, Delaware, Maryland, Pennsylvania, Michigan, California, Indiana, New Jersey.* Liberty, PA, 1970. 19 leaves. [A122; VV].

CHANCE -- Chance, Hilda. *Supplement to Chance of Ohio, Virginia, North Carolina, Georgia, Texas, Tennessee, Kentucky, Delaware, Maryland, Pennsylvania, Michigan, California, Indiana, New Jersey.* Liberty, PA, 1970. [VV].

CHANCELLOR -- Chancellor, Frances Smith. *My Children's Ancestors and Kinfolk.* Owensboro, KY, McDowell Publications, 1981. 237, xxxiii p. Chiefly Genealogical Tables. [D2321].

CHANDLER -- Long, Anne. *Chandlers Found in the 1850 Kentucky Census.* Grangeville, ID, A. Long, 1988. 24p. 1. Chandler family. 2. Kentucky-Genealogy. [G132; NGS4].

CHANDLER -- Sanders, Walter Ray. *The John Chandler Family of Green and Taylor Counties Kentucky.* Litchfield, IL, 1947. 57 l. [L3266; NG29].

CHANDLER -- Walter, Laura T. C. *The Chandler Family: A History of the Chandler Family of Eastern Kentucky.* NP, 1974. 850p. 1. Chandler family. 2. Kentucky-Genealogy. [G132; X-NY].

CHARLES -- Charles, Clell E. *History of the Charles Family in Eastern Kentucky, Southwestern Virginia.* Erwin, TN, 1960. 35p. [S474].

CHARLES -- Vehme, Muriel Branhaur. *History of Charles Family in Eastern Kentucky, Southwest Virginia.* Ft. Washington, MD, Vehme, n.d. 65p. [DC684].

CHASTAIN -- Farnsworth-Milligan, Mary Avilla Abel Hall. *Chastain Kith and Kin, 1700-1980: Revised Chastain Section from 1973 edition of Kith and Kin of Georgia Ridge, Crawford County, Arkansas: with Expansion of Several Branches of Pierre Chastain Descendants.* Owensboro, KY, Cook-McDowell Publishers, 1980. vi, 402p. [C126].

CHEEK -- Cheek, Menifee Reed. *Check Family; The First Cheeks to America and Kentucky.* Nashville, TN, 1965. 54, 7, 3 leaves. [L3352].

CHENOWETH -- Quisenberry, A. C. *Chenoweth Massacre, etc.* Read Before the Kentucky State Historical Society, October 3, 1911. Frankfort, KY, 1911. 59p. [L3360].

CHIPMAN -- Chipman, Everett and Lenore. *Chipmans in Grant County, Kentucky.* NP, n.d., 18p. [X-FW].

CHRISTIAN -- Collins, Anne C. *James and Eliza (Gaines) Collins, Their Siblings, Ancestors, and Descendants: with Information on Related Lines of Christian, Wallace, Pate, Snoddy, and Walker.* United States, A. C. Collins, 1989. xii, 197., 8p. of plates. 1. Collins family, 2. Collins, James, 1821-1891-Family. 3. Collins, Eliza Gaines, 1842-1916-Family. 4. Gaines family. 5. Christian family. 6. Wallace family. [G138].

CHURCHILL -- Todhunter, Charles Timothy. *The Churchill Family Genealogy.* Utica, KY, McDowell Publications, 1988. v. <1- >. 1. Churchill family. 2. Southern States-Genealogy. [G139].

CHURCHMAN -- Churchman, Charles R. *Churchmans of Kentucky.* Louisville, KY, C. R. Churchman, 1988. iv, 288p. 1. Churchman family. 2. Kentucky-Genealogy. [G140].

CLARDY -- Johnson, John W. *A History of the Family of John Collins Clardy of Kentucky.* NP, 1955, 91p. [S496f].

CLARK -- Dorman, John Frederick. *Descendants of General Jonathan Clark, Jefferson County, Kentucky, 1750-1811.* Louisville, KY, 1949. 66p. [NG30].

CLARK -- Thurston, R. C. Ballard. *Clark Family.* Louisville, KY, Thurston & Dorman, 1935, 1936, 1949. 3 v. bound together. [D2505].

CLARK -- Thruston, R. C. B. *Some Recent Findings Regarding the Ancestry of General George Rogers Clark.* Louisville, KY, 1935. 34p. Reprint from the Filson Club History Quarterly.. [X-FW].

CLARKE -- Clark, James W. *Richard Clark of Virginia, 1732-1811, with a Brief History of His Descendants and Their Westward Migration through Montgomery County, Kentucky; Putnam and Montgomery Counties, Indiana; Dallas*

County, Iowa; and Jewell County, Kansas. Abilene, TX, Clark, 1971. 41, 8 l. [D2480; VV].

CLAXTON -- Norris, George W. *Henry Claxton and Descendants 1790-1980.* 2nd Printing. Utica, KY, McDowell, 1989. ix, 766p. [C135; DC737].

CLAY -- Clay, Mary Rogers. *Clay Family; Part First; The Mother of Henry Clay by Hon. Zachary F. Smith...Part Second; The Genealogy of the Clays.* Louisville, KY, J. P. Morton and Company Printer to the Filson Club, 1899. vi, 252, 4p. [L3544].

CLAY -- Nuermberger, Ruth Ketring. *The Clays of Alabama; A Planter-Lawyer Politician Family.* Lexington, KY, U. of Kentucky Press, 1958. 342p. [D2535; X-FW].

CLAY -- Smith, Zachary F. *The Clay Family.* Louisville, KY, John P. Morton and Co., 1899. 252p. [D2536].

CLAYTON -- Harralson, Gwendolene Clayton. *Chronicle of the Clayton Sage on the Occasion of the Clayton Reunion, August 9, 1981, Tirza Primitive Baptist Church, Six Miles North of Providence, Kentucky.* NP, James O. Clayton, 1981. 30 l. [C136; DS125].

CLEMENT -- Clement; Coleman C. Sr. *Genealogical Chart of the Clement Family and Livingston and Crittendon Counties, Kentucky. Rev. 1968.* Atlanta, GA, Clement, 1969. Gen. Table. With 'May of Livingston and Crittendon Counties, Kentucky' by Clement. [S513].

CLEMENTS -- Clements, John Walter Scott. *Origins of Clements - Spalding and Allied Families of Maryland and Kentucky.* Louisville, KY, Clements (Standard Press) 1928. 87p. NG gives 98p. D gives 11, 87p. [L3572; NG30; D2556].

COBB -- Maxie, Marie. *Ambrose Cobb of Lincoln County, North Carolina, Ambrose Cobb* *of Knox County, Kentucky, Vincent Cobb of Jessamine County, Kentucky.* NP, Marie Maxie, 1988. 8 leaves. [DC765].

COBB -- Morgan, Edgar L. *The Cobbs of Owens County, Kentucky.* Louisville, KY, Morgan & Houchens, 1961. 215P. D gives xv, 215, 1 p. [L3634; D2598].

COBURN -- Hoard, Lyon J. *To Kentucky With Boone - The Coburn Family Odyssey.* NP, n.d. 88 leaves. [NG31].

COCHRANE -- Hunter, Miriam M. *The Cochrane Family of Virginia and Kentucky.* Fresno, OH? 1943. 120, 6 leaves. [X-CH/NY; VV].

COFFEY -- Sexton, Jacqueline Coffee... *The Coffeys of Wayne County. 1st ed.* Monticello, KY, Sexton, 1974. 152p. [S523].

COLEMAN -- Coleman, Jonathan. *Descendants of Abraham Coleman and Their Neighbors. Reprint ed.* Pikeville, KY, Pikeville County Historical Society, 1979. 108p. With an added index prepared by Leonard Roberts and Claire Coleman. [C141].

COLEMAN -- Seaman, Catherine Hawes Coleman. *Letters from Migrating Southern Families of the 19th Century: the Letters of Coleman, Harris, and Hawes Families as the Migrate from Virginia to Kentucky, Tennessee, Mississippi, and Arkansas, 1810-1900.* Sweet Briar, VA, Sweet Briar College Printing Press, 1987- v. <1-2 >. 1. Coleman family-Correspondence. 2. Harris family-Correspondence. 3. Hayes family-Correspondence. [G150].

COLEMAN -- Smith, Anetta (C). *Family History of Robert Edward Coleman and His Descendants of Mercer County, Ky,* Harrodsburg, KY, 1969. 76p. [X-FW].

COLLIER -- Collier, Leroy & Mildred English Collier. *Some Collier Families and Folks They're Kin To.* Bowling Green, KY, L. Collier, 1981. 28 l. [C142].

COLLIER -- Collier, Leroy & Mildred (English) Collier. *Descendants of Robert Collier and Isabella Doddington Collier, 1453-1989.* Bowling Green, KY, The Colliers, 1989. 210p. 1. Collier family. 2. Collier, Robert, Ca. 1453-1501-Family. 3. Southern States-Genealogy. [G150].

COLLIER -- Collier, Leroy & Mildred (English) Collier. *Some Collier Families: Descendants of Robert Collier and Isabella Doddington Collier, 1453-1990. 2nd edition.* Bowling Green, KY, The Colliers, 1990. 371p. Rev. ed. of Robert Collier and Isabell Doddington Collier, 1453-1989, 1989. 1. Collier family. 2. Collier, Robert, ca. 1453-1501-Family. 3. Southern States-Genealogy. [G150; DC789].

COLLINS -- Collins, Anne C. [G150]. See above: CHRISTIAN. [G138].

COLLINS -- Hadden, Helen Taylor Collins. *John Collins of Viirginia (sic) and Kentucky: Genealogy and Descendants, 1744-1988.* Paris, KY, House of Heraldry, 1988. 10, 335p. 1. Collins family. 2. Collins, John, 1744-1810-Family. 3. Virginia-Genealogy. 4. Kentucky-Genealogy. [G151].

COLLINS -- Markland, Ruby Collins. *The Jonathan Collins Family and Descendants of Penn., Va., Ky., Tenn., Mo., and Points West.* Provo, UT, J. G. Stevenson, 1969/1970. xii, 236p. [A137].

COLLINS -- Markland, Ruby Collins. *Supplement to The Jonathan Collins Family and Descendants of Penn., Va., (Ky.), Tenn., Mo., and Points West.* Pleasant Grove, UT, R. C. Markland, 1985. 134, xxxiv p., 1 leaf of plates. 1. Collins family, 2. Colins, Jonathan-Family. [G151].

COMBS -- Frazier, Mae. *A Combs Family: Descendants of Shadrack Combs, born 1784-85, Son of John Combs, Jr. born 1761, a*

Revolutionary War Veteran. Lexington, KY, M. Frazier, 1982. 425p. 12 leaves of plates. [C144].

CONNELLY -- Connelly, William Elsey. *Eastern Kentucky Papers: The Founding of Harman's Station, with an Account of the Indian Captivity of Mrs. Jennie Wiley and the Exploration and Settlement of the Big Sandy Valley in the Virginias and Kentucky; to which is Affixed a Brief Account of the Connelly Family and Some of Its Collateral and Related Families in America.* New York, The Torch Press, 1910. 177p. Extracted from a History of Logan County by H. C. Rogland published in the "Logan County Banner" p.87-92. ND. [L3895; D2757; VV].

COOK -- Cook, Doyle. *The Cooks of Dry Creek, KY...* Pennington Gap, VA, Cook, 1988. xv, 206p. [DC820].

COOK -- Goode, Cecil E. [G155]. See above: BEE. [G45].

COOKSEY -- McCurley, James B. *Cooksey of Maryland (1832).* Louisville, KY, J. B. McCurley, 1980. ii, 4 l. [C147].

COOLEY -- Colley, Elizabeth Morrow. *Luther Cooley - Soldier of the American Revolution, 1761-1842.* Fort Thomas, KY, 1966. 9p. [NG32].

COOLEY -- NAS. *Quarterly Bulletin.* Fort Thomas, KY, The Cooley Family Association of America, 1939. DAR Library holdings v.1, no. 1 (1939) - v. 12, no. 4 (1951). Some missing. [D2809].

COOLEY -- NAS. *Cooley Communique.* Ft. Thomas, KY, The Cooley Family Association of America, 1957. _ v. Library Holdings: Vols. 1-2. [DC827].

COOPER -- Cooper, Homer C. *Cooper, McKenny, Ferrell/ Farrell, Woddell, Gothard, Wilson &*

Patton Families of Augusta & Rockbridge Counties, Virginia; York & Adams Counties, Pennsylvania; Blount, Knox, & Roane Counties, Tennessee; Pocahontas, Gilmer & Ritchie Counties, West Virginia; Wayne County, Kentucky; Vigo & Sullivan Counties, Indiana; York County, South Carolina. Athens, GA, 1969. 7 l. [L3990; VV].

COOPER -- Hammers, Marian G. *Some Descendants of Mareen Duvall, the Emigrant, and Allied names, Cooper, Elliott, Fairlie, Blount, Yates, and Piedfort.* Madisonville, KY, M.G.D. Hammers, 1984. 294p. 1 leaf of plates. "The Duvall section of this family history is a supplement to the book, Mareen Duvall of Middle Plantation by Henry Wright Newman, which he had published in 1952. 1. Duvall family. 2. Cooper family. 3. Elliott family. 4. Duvall, Mareen, b. ca.1630-Family. [G156].

CORBLY -- Murphy, Leola Wright. *Sequel to the Life and Times of Reverend John Corbly and Genealogy.* Owensboro, KY, McDowell Publishers, 1982. 242p. 1. Corbly family. [G157; C149].

CORDRY -- Cordry, Eugene Allen. *Descendants of Virginia, Kentucky, and Missouri Pioneers.* Bounceton, MO, Cordry, 1973. xiv, 434p. [D2866].

COSSART -- Cossairt, Joseph Arthur. *The Cossairt Collection, 1180-1935... A Sketch of the following Families, Who are Allied by Marriage. Alcorn, Banta, Duryea, Mount, Van Voorhees, Van Cleef, Van Horn, Van Nest, Rapalie, Montfort, Nevius, Brinkerhoff, De Graff, Terhune, Goelet, Hulick, Demerest, Van Zandt, etc. An Account of the "Low Dutch": Colony on the Raritan, the Connewago, and in Kentucky.* NP, 1935. v. [L4076].

COTTINGHAM -- Atkinson, Frances Halbert. *Cottingham -Dixon Notes.* Greenup, KY, n.d. 3 leaves. [L4080].

COUCH -- Roberts, Leonard. *Up Cutshin & Down Greasy: Folkways of a Kentucky Mountain Family.* Lexington, KY, University Press of Kentucky, 1988. 165p. Originally published in 1959. 1. Kentucky-Social life and customs. 2. Couch family. 3. Folklore-Kentucky. [G160].

COVINGTON -- Covington, Elbert E. *Covington and Kin, 2d ed.* Owensboro, KY, McDowell Publications, 1980. 413p, 5 leaves of plates. [C153].

COWHERD -- Newton, Edythe Cowherd. *Cowherd Genealogy.* Lyndon, KY, Newton, 1962. xii, 407p. [D2959].

COX -- Cox, Bruce K. [G162]. See above: BOGGS. [G65].

COX -- Nacke, Judy. *John W. Sisco & Laura E. Cox and Their Ancestors.* Louisville, KY, J. Nacke, 198_. 53p., 6 p. of plates. 1. Sisco family. 2. Cox family. 3. Graves family. 4. Sisco, John William, 1855-1945-Family. 5. Cox, Laura Edney, 1857-1928-Family. 6. Kentucky-Genealogy. [G162].

COX -- Thacker, Jack H. *Descendants of John Cox, Sr., and Sarah Nunnelly Who were Born in Halifax Co., Va., in 1758, Who Immigrated to Logan Co., Ky., in 1787.* Fairborn, OH, J. H. Thacker, 1986. 109 l. 1. Cox family. 2. Cox, John, 1758-1832-Family. 3. Kentucky-Genealogy. [G162].

CRADDOCK -- Craddock, Rebecca Susan. *"Craddock Cousins" Then and Now: A Family History of John Craddock of Hart County, Kentucky, with a Collection of Nots on Other Craddocks in Kentucky and Other States.* __, KY, S. C. Lafferty, 1986. a-f, 198 l. 1. Craddock family. 2. Craddock, John, ca.1763-1853-Family. 3. Kentucky -Genealogy. [G163].

CRADY -- Adams, Evelyn Crady. *David Crady, Kentucky Pioneer.* NP, Walter Crady, 1947. 24 leaves. [D2987].

CRAFT -- Collier, Joella Craft. *A Family Called Craft.* Pikeville, KY, (Craft Family Reunion Association) Printing by George, 1985. ii, 204p. 1. Craft family. 2. North Carolina-Genealogy. [G163; C155].

CRAIG -- Craig, Mrs. William. *Taliaferro Craig Family of Virginia and Kentucky.* Hartford City, IN. [VV].

CRAIG -- Miller, Caroline R. *The Bath County, Kentucky Craigs' Ancestors and Descendants, 1703-1982: A Working Paper Designed to Further Research in Celebration of the Craig Reunion Held July 18, 1982, Frenchburg, Kentucky.* Augusta, KY, C. R. Miller, 1982. 42p. 2 p. of plates. [C155].

CRANE -- Crain, Luther N. Sr. and Mary Alice Stinson Crain. *Descendants of John G. Crain, Boyle County, Kentucky and Descendants of John W. Stinson, Hart County, Kentucky. Rev ed.* Louisville, KY, L. N. Crain, 1982. 125p. [C156].

CRANE -- Crain, Luther N. Sr. and Mary Alice Stinson Crain. *Descendants of John G. Crain, Boyle County, Kentucky and Descendants of John W. Stinson, Hart County, Kentucky: Also, California Crane Connection - Rev. -* Louisville, KY, 1983. 145p. 1. Crane family. 2. Stimson family. 3. Crain, John G., 1808-1872. 4. Stinson, John W., 1822-1907-Family. 5. Kentucky-Genealogy. [G163; C157].

CRANE -- Crain, Luther N. Sr. and Mary Alice Stinson Crain. *Descendants of John G. Crain, Boyle County, Kentucky and Descendants of John W. Stinson, Hart County, Kentucky: Also, California Crane Connection. Rev. 1985.* Louisville, KY, 1985. 234p. [C157].

CRANE -- Crain, Luther N. Sr. and Mary Alice Stinson Crain. *Descendants of John G. Crain, Boyle County, Kentucky and Descendants of John W. Stinson, Hart County, Kentucky: Also, California Crane Connection - Rev. 1986 -*

Louisville, KY, 1986. 235p. 1. Crane family. 2. Stinson family. 3. Crain, John G., 1808-1872. 4. Stinson, John W., 1822-1907-Family. 5. Kentucky-Genealogy. [G163].

CRAVEN -- Craven, Patricia. *The Craven Clan of Southwestern Pennsylvania and Various Kentucky Counties.* Chicago, Craven, 1988. 101p. [DC871].

CRAWFORD -- Crawford, John Leland. *Whence We Came.* Corbin, KY, The Corbin Times Tribune, Inc., 1941. 2, 7-47p. [L4221].

CREECH -- NAS. *One Mans Cravin'...* Pine Mountain, KY, Pine Mountain Settlement School, 1945. 49p. 100th Anniversary of the Birth of William Creech and Sally Dixon Creech. [X-FW].

CREECH -- Creech, Lillian Broughton. *Creech Lineage.* Baltimore, MD, Gateway Press, 1989. 593, liv p., 7 pages. of plates. 1. Creech family. 2. Kentucky-Genealogy. [G164].

CREECH -- Lloyd, Dean. *Larsh Creech and Joseph Wynn Family Tree.* Morehead, KY, 1964. 12p. [S586].

CREEKMORE -- Bowman, Anna Harman. *Some Kentuckians Move West: Creekmores, Blakelys and Related Families.* Oklahoma City, OK, 1970. ii, 80p. [A161].

CROCKETT -- Hill, Dorothy V. *The Crockett, Davidson (Davison), Graham, Montgomery, Stockton and Allied Families of Virginia, Kentucky and Missouri, also the Taylor - Hill and March - Cureton Families of Virginia - Ohio - New England - Alabama - California.* NP, 1969. 108 l. [D3078: VV].

CROCKETT -- French, J. P. C. *Davy Crockett and the Crockett Family.* Chatanooga, TN, Lookout Pub., 1951. 25p. [X-FW].

CROCKETT -- Price, Samuel W. *Biographical Sketch of Colonel Joseph Crockett; A Paper*

Read befor the Filson Club, 1908. Louisville, KY, 1909, 85p. (Filson Club Publ. no. 24, pt. 2). [X-FW].

CROCKETT -- Torrence, Robert M. *Colonel "Davy" Crockett.* Washington, DC, H. Fagan, 1956. 23p. [X-NY/PH]

CROMER -- Sparkman, Jan. *Our Fathers Before Us: A Family Journal. Cromer Family.* Berea, KY, 1980. 115p. [NG34].

CROMWELL -- Waylen, James. *Cecil County Cromwells, and Their Offshoot in Kentucky.* NP, 189_. Pages not shown. [L4279].

CROSS -- Coles, James E. *The Vaughn/Cross Family Book.* Paducah, KY, J. E. Coles, 1989. 267, A-D p. 1. Vaughn family. 2. Cross family. 3. Arkansas-Genealogy. [G167].

CROSS -- Cross, John Newton & Mary Cross Cole. *William Cross of Botetourt Co., Va., and His Descendants, 1733-1932, also a Record of the Related Families of McCown, Gentry - Blythe, Cain - Robertson, Harris - Martin, and Conner of Virginia, Kentucky, Illinois, and Missouri.* Columbia, MO, E. W. Stephens Pub. Co., 1932. 258p. [L4309; D3098; VV].

CROUCH -- Roberts, Leonard. *Sang Branch Settlers; Folksongs and Tales of a Kentucky Mountain Family. Music Transcribed by C. Buell Agey.* Austin, TX, Published for the American Folklore Society by the University of Texas Press. 1974. xxi, 401p. (Publications of the American Folklore Society, Memoir series; v. 61). 1. Folk songs, English-Kentucky-History and criticism. 2. Folklore-Kentucky. 3. Tales-Kentucky. 4. Kentucky-Social life and customs. 5 Crouch family. 6. Mountain whites (Southern States). 7. Folk music-Kentucky. [G167].

CROWELL -- Crowell, Billy Frazier. *Ancestors and Descendants of John Jackson Crowell.* Paducah, KY, B. F. Crowell, 1990.

81, A-M, 2 leaves. 1. Crowell family. 2. Crowell, John Jackson, 1877-1963-Family. 3. Southern States-Genealogy. [G167].

CULBERTSON -- Dixon, Ben F. *The Family of David Culbertson of Lincoln County, KY.* NP, 1963. 37 leaves. [D3132].

CULBERTSON -- Dixon, Benjamin F. *The Family of David Culbertson of Lincoln County, Kentucky; An Historical and Genealogical Study.* San Diego, CA, 1963. n.d., 39p. [X-FW].

CULLEN -- Paris, Amy. *The Paris Family: Including Cullen, Heavrin, and Mackey Lines.* Utica, KY, McDowell Publications, 1984. 124p. 1. Paris family. 2. Cullen family. 3. McKee family. [G168].

CUNNINGHAM -- Gingles, Bertie C. *History and Genealogy of William Cunningham and His Wife Nancy (Carr) Cunningham.* Murray, KY, Murray Democrat Publishing Co., 1957. 431p. [L4378; D3157].

CUMMINS -- Funk, Frances (Roach). *Cummins Ancient, Cummins, New; A History of the Cummins Family of Rockcastle Co., Kentucky.* Washington, DC, 1978. 326p. [NG34].

CUMMINS -- Funk, Frances. *Cummins Ancient, Cummins New. Cummins Family of Rockcastle County, Ky.* Washington, DC, 1980. 2 v. 326p. C lists under CUMMINGS and shows no date or place of publication. [C162; NG34].

CURD -- James, Jessamine Bland. *Curd Family Records of Kentucky Branch. 1949-1970,* NP, 3 v. bound together. [D3163].

CURD -- Neal, Harley Buntin. *Captain John Curd, Kentucky Pioneer - 1st ed.* - Rockford, IL, H. B. Neal, 1990. x, 45 l. 1. Curd family. 2. Curd, John, b.1726-Family. 3. Kentucky-Genealogy. 4. Virginia-Genealogy. [G169].

CURRENT -- Hall, Martha Belle; Rion, Myrtle; and McCann, William R. *Family of Matthew Current Who Married Jane Wilson Call.* Paris, Bourbon County, KY. , 1955. 15p. [NG34].

CURRENT -- Endicott, Pattye Current. *Some Descendants of John Current of Bourbon County, Kentucky.* Cynthiana, KY, Endicott, 1957. 43, vi p. [D3169].

D

DALE -- Daniels, Almon E. *A Work Book on the Dale Families of Virginia, with Particular Reference to the Branch Which Moved From the Northern Neck of Virginia to Woodford County, Kentucky, and with Notes on the Related Families of Dodson, Goad, Hanks, Phillips, Syndor, etc.* Arlington, VA, 1958. 1 vol. (unpaged). Genealogical. Table. [X-FW/LA/NY; VV].

DALLOW -- Dallow, Charles H. *Dallow Family.* Ft. Thomas, KY, 11p. [X-FW].

DAMERON -- Dameron, Alfred Speer. *Historical and Genealogical Sketch of of the Dameron Family of England and Virginia.* Newport, KY, 1940. [VV].

DARNELL -- Twain, Mark. *The Grangerford - Shepherdson Feud; Facsimile of that Episode's First Publication Prior to Adventures of Huckleberry Finn, with an Account of Mark Twain's use of the Bloddy Encounters at Compromise Kentucky by Edgar Marquess Branch & Robert H. Hurst.* Berkeley, CA, Friends of the Bancroft Library, University of California, 1985. 91p. (No. 33 in a series of keepsakes issued by the Friends of the Bancroft Library for its members. 1. Mark Twain, 1835-1910. Adventures of Hucklebarry Finn. 2. Darnell family. 3. Watson family. 4. Vendetta in literature. 5. Vendetta-Tennessee. 6. Vendetta-Kentucky. [G175].

DAUGHHETTE -- Heinemann, Charles Brunk. *The Daughhette Family of Estell (sic) County, Kentucky*. Washington, DC, 1933. 26, 8 numb. leaves. [L4561].

DAUGHHETTE -- Heinemann, Charles Brunk. *The Daughhette Family of Estill County, Kentucky*. Big Laurel, VA, 1934. [VV].

DAUGHHETTE -- Heinemann, Charles Brunk. *The Daughhette Family of Frederick, Shenandoah, and Monongalia Counties, Va.; Clark and Estill Counties, Ky.; Cape Girardeau County, Mo.; and Other Locations indicated in the compilation*. Washington, DC, 1935. 90 l. [L4562;VV].

DAVID -- David, Harold T. *William H. David, Kentucky Pioneer*. Cleveland, KY, David, 1976. 73p. [C170; D3295].

DAVIDSON -- Davidson, Selden. *Eastern Kentucky Davidsons*. Ashland, KY, S. Davidson, 1984. 111 p. 6 pages of plates. [C171].

DAVIS -- Berndt, Betty Jean Davis. *Davis: Jesse Buford Davis, 1845 Ky. - 1928 Mo; His Descendants, Ancestors, Some Connecting Families*. Kansas City, MO?, 1973. iv, 348p. [S637].

DAVIS -- Davis, W. E. *The Davis Family: Joseph, Ellenor (Lewis), Mathias, Richard, etc*. Glendale, OH, W. E. Davis. 1985. 1 v. (various foliations). 1. Davis family. 2. Kentucky-Genealogy. 3, Davis, Joseph, b. ca. 1770-Family. [G177].

DAVIS -- DeVerter, Ruth Hendricks. *The Genealogy of the Davis Family, Middlesex County, Virginia, and Montgomery County, Kentucky*. Baytown, TX, 1957. [VV].

DAVIS -- Dickinson, Mrs. Ollie. *Notes on the Genealogy of the Davis, Mace-Richey Families of North Carolina, Kentucky and Iowa*. NP, n.d. 6 leaves. [X-LA].

DAVIS -- Harris, Mayme Ellen Fisher. *Davis, Price, Dezarn, Bell, Pierce, Skaggs, Saltsman, Warren, and Allied Lines in Green Co., Ky.* Chicago Heights, IL, DAR, 1962. 129 leaves. [D3342; X-FW].

DAVIS -- Hoffman, Muriel M. M. *Family of Jeremiah and Cassandra Elizabeth Gum Davis, Green County, Ky., Cass County, Ill.* Alton, IL, 1970. 47p. [X-FW].

DAVIS -- Watson, Gary Wayne. *Descdants of Edward Davis of Mercer County, Kentucky: The First Five Generations.* Urbana, IL?, G. W. Watson, 1985. 447p. [DC967].

DAWKINS -- Prewitt, Lela Wolfe. *The Dawkins and Stewart Families of Virginia and Kentucky.* Fairfield, IA. Stewart, 1968. vi, 154p. [L4658; D3371; VV].

DAWSON -- Mills, Harry Willard. *Dawson Family History; Descendants of Elijah Dawson, sr., and Sarah (Logan) Dawson of Lincoln County, Kentucky.* Washington, DC, 1941. 16 leaves. [L4663].

DAY -- Carby, Lorenza Duncan. *The Joseph Day Family of Grayson County, Ky.* Highland, CA, R. W. Fentress, 1981. 82 l. 1. Day family. 2. Grayson County (Ky,)-Genealogy. [G179].

DAY -- McGivney, Vivian and Mrs. Ken (Vivian) Nogle. *Third Supplement to the Descendants of Robert Day of Hartford, Connecticut and Captain John Day, Number 194, of Sheffield, Ohio and Alfred Day of Mondovi, Wisconsin, 1978 ed.* Hartford, KY, McDowell Publications, 1978. 81, 77p. Includes reprint of portions of: A genealogical register of the Descendants in the male line of Robert Day. G. E. Day, 2d ed. Northampton, OH, printed by J. & L. Metcalf. 1858. [C174].

DEAN -- Coak, Dorothy Putnam. *Dean - Lamb Memorabilia: Compiled for Deanwood's Celebration of July 4th, 1976.* Deanwood, KY, Coak, 1976. 527p. [C175].dixon

DEARINGER -- Dearinger, David B. *Descendants of William Dearinger of Owen County, Kentucky.* NY, NY, 1973. 66p. [X-FW].

DECKER -- Downs, Barry W. *The Decker Family of Grayson County, Kentucky.* Leichtfield, KY, B. W. Downs, 1986. x, 202p. 1. Decker family. 2. Kentucky-Genealogy. [G182].

DECKER -- Mallisee, Natalia Decker. *Barnett Decker, 1778-1838: History and Genealogy.* Leichtfield, KY, N. D. Mallisee, 1984. 131p. 1. Decker family. 2. Decker, Barnett, 1778-1838-Family. [G183].

DEDMAN -- Griffith, Anna Laura (Deadmon). *Dedman - Deadmon Family History.* Mayfield, KY, A. L. Griffith, 1983. iv, 153p. [C176].

DEHOFF -- McCurley, James B. *Dehoff (Dahuff, Dehoof, Dehooff, or Dehuff, later Dahoff, Dayhoff, Dayhuff, Deahofe, or De Hoff) Pennsylvania (1757): Preliminary Outline of the Family (Only partially verified).* Louisville, KY, J. B. McCurley, 1980. xiv, 7 leaves. [C177; VP].

DeLONG -- NAS. *DeLong - Tucker Families.* NP, Kentucky DAR, G.R.C. 1967-68. 263 leaves. [D3474].

DeLONG -- DeLong, Edmund S. *Kentucky Branch of the De Long Family.* Princeton, NJ, 1970. 38p. [X-FW].

DEVINE -- Bailey, Jack Dalton. *Bury Me at Dixville: A Genealogical Research of the Descendants of I - Armstead Patterson, II - John Divine (Devine), III - John Leonard, IV - Samuel Bugg.* Harrodsburg, KY, J. D. Bailey, 1985. 119p. 1. Patterson family. 2. Devine family. 3. Leonard family. 4. Kentucky-Genealogy. [G187].

DEWEESE -- Deweese, Raymond P & Catherine Caroline. *The Deweese's [sic] of Butler*

County, Kentucky: The Trail Leading Westward. NP, The Authors, 1988. 430p. [DC1025].

DE YOUNG -- Roper, Mary Louise Gaw. *The Gaw, De Young, Hudiburg, Williams, and Allied Families - 1st ed.* - Utica, KY, McDowell Publications, c1987. xiv, 257p. 1. Gaw family. 2. De Young family. 3. Hudiburgh family. 4. Williams family. [G181].

DICK -- Hickam, Nora Tomasine Jones. *The Family of John R. Dick of Wayne County, Kentucky.* Evansville, IN, Hickam, 1987. 71, 6 l. [DC1030].

DICKERSON -- Cox, Carlyle E. *Diskerson, A Kentucky-Virginia Family.* Chicago, IL, 1938. 48 l. [L4927; VV].

DICKINSON -- Ward, Clare McVickar. *Analysis is of the Dickinson Family of Virginia and Kentucky.* NP, 1974. 2 v. [NG37].

DILLARD -- Haemmel, William G. *The Tidewater Virginia Dillards and Kin: Some of the Descendants of George Dillard, c1625-? Who Arrived in Virginia in c1640 and Some Generations of Other Family Lines and Additional Ancestral Lines.* Utica, KY, McDowell Publications, 1985. 339p., 4 p. of plates. 1. Dillard family. 2. Dillard, George, b. ca. 1625-Family. 3. Virginia-Genealogy. [G191].

DINWIDDIE -- DeVerter, Ruth (Hendricks). *The Duncan and Dinwiddie Families with Allied Lines; Scotland; Virginia; Shelby, Boone and Bourbon Counties, Kentucky; Rush and Hendricks Counties, Indiana, and Westward Migrants as far as California.* Baytown, TX, 1969. xii, 211 leaves. [A187].

DIXON -- Richards, Mary Ellen. *The Dixons of Allen County, Kentucky.* NP, Richards, 19__. 39 leaves. [D3643].

DIXON -- Sample, Trixie Dixon. *Dixons, From Virginia to Texas.* Owensboro, KY, Cook-McDowell Publications, 1981. 12, 111, 9p., 11 leaves of plates. Rev. ed. of Dixons from Virginia to Texas compiled by E. P. Scott, 197_. [C186; VV].

DOMINY -- Claxton, Lanell Dominy. *Our Kin Dominy-Duncan-Ellington-Fordham-Miller.* Utica, KY, McDowell Publications, Hazelhurst, GA, L. D. Claxton, 1989. xi, 490p. 1. Dominy family. 2. Duncan family. 3. Ellington family. 4. Georgia-Genealogy. [G195].

DONAHUE -- Young, Laurie. *Notes on Keith, Lott, Donahoo, and Sketoe Families of Early Muhlenberg County, Kentucky.* Boise, ID, L. Young, 1989. 140p. 1. Keith family. 2. Lott family. 3. Donahue family. 4. Sketoe family. 5. Kentucky-Genealogy. 6. Muhlenberg County (Ky.)-Genealogy. [G195].

DONALDSON -- Donaldson, O. Clyde. *Heritage and History and Geneology of the Donaldson and Whaley Families of Bath County, Kentucky and Their Descendants.* Hopkins, MN, Donaldson, 1979. 196p. 1 leaf of plates. [C188].

DONAN -- Patchett, Frances Donan. *David Crewes Donan of Kentucky and His Family.* Chicago, IL, Adams Press, 1977. iv, 195p. [DS190].

DOOLEY -- Cline, Laura Smith. *Dooley and Scobee Families in Virginia, Kentucky, and Missouri. Rev.* Los Altos, CA, 1982. iii, 73p. [C189; VV].

DOUGLAS -- Harris, Ruthe Eleanor Poole. *Ruth Eleaner Douglas Journal: with Genealogies of Douglas, Noell, Callaway, Clemens, Moorman, and Other Related Bedford County, Virginia Families: Also Genealogies of Douglas Families of Tennessee, Kentucky, Missouri.* Nashville, TN, Douglas Family Publishers, 1979 - v. [C191; VV].

DOWELL -- Cox, Opal London. [G198]. See above: BEWLEY. [G54].

DOWNING -- Downing, Juanita M. H. *The Benjamin Downing, Sr., Family, 1775-1980.* Louisville, KY, Downing, 1982. p. 100-250. Supplement and Index, 1982. [C191].

DRAKE -- Isaac, Sallie Carr Drake. *The Story of Drakesboro and Its Founders.* Drakesboro, KY, S.C.D. Isaac, 1952. 1. Drakesboro (Ky,)-History. 2. Drake family. [G199].

DUDDERAR -- Newborg, Ruth Foxx. *The Dudderars From Germany to Kentucky.* NP, 1983. 127 leaves. [DS202].

DUFF -- Barnett, James D. *John Duff of North Ireland, Virginia and Kentucky and His Descendants.* NP, 1935. [VV].

DUFFNER -- Cain, Marilyn Wright Duffner. [G203]. See above: BOEDECKER. [G64].

DUNCAN -- Ardery, Julia Hoge (Spencer). *The Duncans of Bourbon County, Kentucky.* Lexington, KY, W. S. Welsh Printing Company, 1943. 27, 1p. [L5281; NG38; D3822].

DUNCAN -- Claxton, Lanell Dominy. [G203]. See above: DOMINY. [G195].

DUNCAN -- Fitzgerald, Anne L. *Duncan Family Data, 1750-1900, Boone County and Scott County, Kentucky.* NP, 1957. 23 l. [D3825].

DUNCAN -- Vick, Velma B. *The Duncans of Culpeper County, Virginia to Logan County, Kentucky.* NP, 1954. 157 l. [D3828; VV].

DUNLAP -- Caraway, William Oates. *Genealogy, Descendants of Alexander Dunlap including Hodge - Atchison - Crockett - Rice - Bailey - Hazelrigg - Richards - Wyatt and Allied Families - Early Virginia and Kentucky Pioneers.* Sugar Land, TX, Caraway, 1956. 40 leaves. [D3838; VV].

DUNN -- Dunn, Gerald C. *1850 Va. Census, Surname Dunn.* Edgewood, KY, G. C. Dunn, 1988. 14, 14, 2, 2, leaves. 1. Dunn family. 2. Virginia-Genealogy. [G204].

DUNN -- Dunn, Gerald C. *Dunn Genealogical Records.* Edgewood, KY, <1986- >. v. <1-13 > in <3 >. 1. Dunn family-Indexes. [G204].

DUNN -- Dunn, William Edward. *The James McMurry Dunn Family of Texas and Kentucky.* NP, 124p. [D3845].

DUPUY -- Dupuy, Rev. B. H. *The Huguenot Bartholomew Dupuy and His Descendants.* Louisville, KY, Courier-Journal Job Printing Co., 1908. xvi, 439, 1p. [L5344; D3860].

DURBIN -- Cox, Pearl Mix. *Durbin - Witt - Wagers, Richardson - Stephens and Related Families via Maryland, Virginia, Kentucky, Missouri.* Warrensburg, MO, P. M. Cox, 1987. xi, 687p. 1. Durbin family. 2. Witt family. 3. Weger family. [G205].

DuVAL -- Buchann, Margaret Gwin. *DuVals of Kentucky from Virginia, 1794-1935, Descendants and Allied Families.* Lynchburg, VA, J. P. Bell Co., 1937. xv, 265p. [L5366; D3883; VV].

DUVALL -- Hammers, Marian G. [G205]. See above: COOPER. [G156].

DUVALL -- Harris, Hugh Henry and Katherine F. *The Duvall, Doyle, and Harris Families with Related Families.* Hartford, KY, McDowell Publications, 1979. 165p. [C200].

DUVALL -- Small, Calvert P. *The Duvall Family in Livingston and Crittendon Counties, Kentucky.* Marion KY, Small, Small, 1973. 42 leaves. [D3887].

DYER -- Arnold, Jane D. *John Mason Dyer Family of Union County, Kentucky, Ancestors and Descendants.* Franklin, KY, 1972 152p. [X-FW].

E

EARLY -- Early, Cleland Edward. *The Early Families of Knox and Whitley Counties, Kentucky and Allied Families.* Houston, TX, D. Armstrong, Co., 1989. 231p., xxvii p. of plates. 1. Early family. 2. Kentucky-Genealogy. [G207; DC1139].

EARP -- Earp, Charles Albert & Williams, Irmalee Earp. *The Joshua Earp Family of Maryland, Kentucky and Ohio.* NP, The Authors, 1990. 6 l. [DC1140].

EASLEY -- O'Brien, Bobbie Hamilton. *John Mayberry Easley, His Ancestors and Descendants, 1818-1978.* Hartford, KY, McDowell Publications, 1978. viii, 242p. [C203].

EDGE -- Hamilton, Anna. *The Genealogy of the John Edge Family, 1683-1986.* Whitesville, KY, A. L. Hamilton, 1986. 183p. 1. Edge family. 2. Edge, John, fl. 1681-1700-Family. [G208].

EDMISTON -- Edmiston, Carroll Evan. *Our Families From the Atlantic Coast Colonies of 1665 to the California Pacific of 1974.* Danville, KY, Edmiston, 1974. 156p. [S766; D3976].

EDMUNDS -- Thompson, Alice Chapman. *The Edmunds and Barton Families of Virginia and Kentucky.* NP, 1978. 50 leaves. [D3983; VV].

EDWARDS -- NAS. *Old Wills From Virginia, Kentucky, Maryland.* ___, MO, DAR, G. R. C., 1951. 23 leaves. [D4006; VV].

EDWARDS -- Crabb, Opal Cline. *Henry Skeggs, Longhunter and the Captain Cader Edwards Family, 1765-1820.* Calhoun, KY, O. C. Crobb, 1978. 87p. 1. Skeggs, Henry, d. ca. 1820-Friends and associates. 2. Edwards family. 3. Kentucky-Biography. 4. Pioneers-Kentucky-History. [G208].

EDWARDS -- Edwards, Cyrus. *The Edwards Family of Barren County, Kentucky, History and Traditions. An Account of the Life and Services of Captain Cader Edwards... with Some Mention of His Numerous Descendants.* Louisville, KY, Press of G. G. Fetter company, inc., Horse Cave, KY, Edwards, 1924. 88p. [L5506; D3995].

EDWARDS -- Edwards, Georgie H. *Historical Sketches of the Edwards and Todd Families and Their Descendants, 1523-1895...* Lexington, KY, Univ. of KY Library, 1964. Pages not given. Reprint of 1894 ed. Library of Congress has original. [X-DP/LA].

EDWARDS -- Edwards, Richard Laurence. *Ancestors and Decendants of the Edwards - Mathias, Delozier, and Related Families that Pioneered through Virginia, Carolinas, Tennessee, Kentucky, Illinois, Missouri, Kansas, and spread to Descendants in Thirty-Seven States and Two Provinces in Canada - 1st ed. -* Coffeyville, KS, R. L. Edwards, 1985. xvi, 597p. 1. Edwards family. 2. Mathis family. 3. Delozier family. [G208; C205; VV].

ELKIN -- Heinemann, Charles Brunk. *James Elkin Family of Clark County, Kentucky.* Washington, DC, 1931. 2p., 14, 5 numb l. [L5581].

ELLINGTON -- Claxton, Lanell Dominy. [G211]. See above: DOMINY. [G195].

ELLIOTT -- Hammers, Marian G. [G212]. See above: COOPER. [G156].

ELLIOTT -- NAS. *Family History of Families From Connecticut, Delaware, New Jersey, Virginia, Kentucky.* __, IN? Indiana DAR, G.R.C., 1949. 109 l. [D4058].

ELLIS -- Cornelius-Koprowski, Mary. *The Family of Garrett W. Ellis, Martha Craine Ellis, and Descendants.* Taylorsville, KY, M. Cornelius-Koprowski, 1985. 160 l. 1. Ellis family. 2. Ellis, Garrett W., d. 1841- - Family. [G212].

ELLIS -- Ellis, Dorothy. *The Ellis Family.* Pewee Valley, KY, Ellis, Ellis, 1980. 37 l. [D4064].

ELMORE -- Cash, Ben LeGrande. *Roberts and Elmore: Being a Record of the Families of Lewis Roberts of Newcomerstown, Ohio and of Hardin Henry Elmore of Kentucky and Loami, Illinois.* Albuquerque, NM, B. L. Cash, 1986. 40 leaves. 1. Roberts family. 2. Elmore family. 3. Roberts, Lewis, 1796-1857-Family, 4. Elmore, Hardin, Henry, 1813-1902-Family. [G213].

ELMORE -- Elmore William E. *"Elmore Papers": Concerning the Early Elmores in Virginia, North Carolina, with Some Information Regarding S. C. and Ky. Early Elmores.* Phoenix, AZ, M. Elmore, 1983. 106 leaves. [C210; VV].

ELSWICK -- Elswick, Jeanette. *Elswick Genealogy: A Genealogical Record of the Elswick Family, 1784-1900; Early Settlers of Buchanan County, Virginia, Pike County, Kentucky and Their Descendants.* Elkhorn City, KY, Elswick, 1973. 40 leaves. [D4092; VV].

ELSWICK -- Elswick, Jeanette. *Elswick Genealogy: A Genealogical Record of the Elswick Family, 1784-1900; Early Settlers of Buchanan County, Virginia, Pike County, Kentucky and Their Descendants.* Elkhorn City, KY, 1973. 2, 14 l. [S792].

EMBREY -- Crawford, Maydee. *Embry.* ___, KY, C. Maydee (sic) 1990. 176p. 1. Embrey family. 2. Kentucky-Genealogy. [G213].

ENGLAND -- England, Ernest J. *The Descendants of Jonathan England of Adair County, Kentucky.* Cape Coral, FL, E. J. England, 1979. 115, a-q p. [C213].

ENGLISH -- Collier, Leroy. *Thomas English and Descendants and Some of Their Kin.* Bowling Green, KY, L. and M. Collier, 1986. 165p. 1. English family. 2. English, Thomas, d. 1664-Family. 3. Tennessee-Genealogy. [G215].

ESTES -- Nelson, Doris. *Following the Chism Estes Trail. A Genealogy of Chism Estes of His Descendants, 1736-1982.* Owensboro, KY, McDowell Publications, 1982. iii, 246p. [C215].

ETCHISON -- Barekman, June B. *History of Edmund Etchison, Revolutionary Soldier of North Carolina, and His Descendants: Including Atchisons--Virginia, Maryland, Kentucky--and Records of...Kin Throughout America.* Chicago, IL, J. Barekman, 1980. 264p. 3 l. of plates. [C215; VV].

F

FEE -- McGroarty, Wm. B. *Fee Family in Maryland, Pennsylvania, Kentucky & Ohio, 1703-1944.* Alexandria, VA, 1944. 20p. [X-FW; VP].

FELTNER -- Feltner, Conrad W. *The Feltner Family.* Middlesboro, KY, C. W. Feltner, 1979. ii, 730p. [C224].

FELTNER -- Feltner, Conrad W. *Völkner Family Letters.* Middlesboro, KY, C. W. Feltner, 1981. xv, 347 leaves. [C224].

FENTRESS -- Carby, Lorenza Duncan. *William Fentress Family of Grayson Co., Ky.* Yucaipa, CA, Randall W. Fentress, 1985. 111 leaves. 1. Fentress family. 2. Fentress, William, 1791-1848-Family. 3. Grayson County (Ky.)-Genealogy. [G226].

FESSLER -- Fessler, William T. *Fessler Ancestories: Foreign Origins and Family Summaries and Briefs in Pennsylvania: Also Briefs in California, Illinois, Indiana, Iowa,*

Kansas, Kentucky, North Carolina, Missouri, Ohio, Virginia: Plus Hundreds of Other Surnames. Haddonfield, NJ, 1980. [VV].

FILSON -- Durrett, Reuben T. *John Filson, the First Historian of Kentucky.* Louisville, KY, John P. Morton & Co., Printer, 1884. 132p. [D4382].

FISHBACK -- Fishback, James. *Genealogy of the John Fishback Family of Culpepper, Virginia.* Glasgow, KY, Press of the Republican, 1912. 31p. [X-CH].

FISHER -- Fisher, Margaret. *The Fisher Line.* Owensboro, KY, Cook & McDowell Publications, 1980. 377, 27p., 50 pages of plates. D shows 450p. [C229; D4412].

FISHER -- Fisher, Mayme E. *Fisher Families of Pennsylvania, Virginia, Kentucky.* Chicago Heights, IL, D. A. R. Saulk Trail Chapter, 1964. 219p. [X-FW; VP].

FISHER -- Fisher, Philip A. *Fisher Families of Penna.- Virginia - Kentucky.* NP, 1964. 244 leaves. [D4413; VV].

FISHER -- Heinemann, C. B. *Ludwig (Lewis) Fisher Family of Virginia and Kentucky.* NP, 1964. [VV].

FITCH -- Lewis, Ailene Fitch. *Fitch, Crawford, Davis, McFarland Francis, Holderman and Allied Lines from Pennsylvania, Tennessee, Kentucky, North Carolina, Illinois to Johnson County, Missouri; 1722-1971.* Holden, MO, Lewis, 1971. 42 leaves. [X-NY].

FITCH -- Lewis, Ailene Fitch. *Fitch, Crawford, Davis, Holderman, Francis, McFarland and Allied Lines from Pennsylvania, Tennessee, Kentucky, North Carolina, Illinois to Johnson County, Missouri; 1722-1976.* Holden, MO, Lewis, 1976. 130p. [D4438; VP].

FITZHUGH -- Elkins, Mary T. *History of Fitzhughes (sic) in England and America;*

Virginia, Kentucky, Missouri and Oregon. Sherman Oaks, CA, 1956. [VV].

FITZSIMMONS -- Hathaway, Bernice (FitzSimmons). *The FitzSimmons and Allied Lines: Ellis, Lee, Perkins, Radford, Redding, Aston, Cocke, Smith, Pierce. Some of the Ancestors and All of the Descendants of Willis FitzSimmons b. 1854, d. 1930: Early Virginia and Kentucky Lines.* Denver, CO, 1963. 108p. [L6130].

FLEENOR -- Fleenor, James R. *Fleenor.* Richmond, KY, Fleenor, 1976. 173p. [D4464].

FLEET -- Fleet, Benjamin Robert. *Green Mount.* Lexington, KY, University of Kentucky Press, 1962. xxiv, 37p. [D4467].

FLOYD -- Floyd, N. J. *Biographical Genealogies of the Virginia-Kentucky Floyd Family, with Notes on Some Collateral Branches.* Baltimore, William and Wilkins Company, 1912. 113p. [L6190; D4514; VV].

FOGG -- Lee, Lillian Fogg. *The Fogg Family of Ingham County, Michigan from 1882-1967, with Prologue and Index: Included is Information on Related Kentucky, New England, and New York Families.* Glendale, CA, 1966. 46p. [L6198].

FOLEY -- Foley, Mary Donna. *The Foley Family of Southern KY: Descendants of Spencer & Nancy Rector Foley.* Russell Springs, KY, M.D. Foley, 1988. 215p. 1. Foley family. 2. Foley, Spencer, b. 1785-Family. 3. Kentucky-Genealogy. [G234].

FORD -- Cain, Stith Malone. *A History of Our Ford Family of Virginia, Kentucky, Indiana, Mississippi, Missouri, and Tennessee.* Whitewater, WI, Cain, 1971. 82 leaves. [S886; D4550; VV].

FORD -- Emberson, Myrtle T. *Notes on Ford... Kentucky.* Los Angeles, CA, 1937. Unpaged. [X-LA].

FORD -- Leslie, E. Glen. *Crittenden Cousins: the History and Genealogy of the Horning, Ford, and Vaughn Families.* Utica, KY, McDowell Publications, 1986. v, 224p. 1. Horning family. 2. Ford family. 3. Vaughn family. 4. Crittendon County (Ky.)-Genealogy. [G235].

FORD -- Wulfeck, Dorothy F. *Ford Families of Virginia and Kentucky.* Naugatuck, CT, 1974. iv, 64, 10, 13p. [X-FW/PH; VV].

FOSTER -- Denham, Marion Lee. *Stewarts, Forresters, and Related Families of Muhlenberg County, Kentucky: A History of the Ancestry and Descendants of Eli Stewart and Sara Lelia Forrester.* Henderson, KY, M. L. Denham, 1987. xxv, 315p. 1. Stuart family. 2. Foster family. 3. Stewart, Eli, 1882-1962-Family. 4. Stewart, Sarah Lelia, 1887-1964-Family. 5. Kentucky-Genealogy. [G236].

FOWLER -- Arthur, Glenn Dora Fowler (Mrs. James Joyce Arthur. *Annals of the Fowler Family with Branches in Virginia, North Carolina, South Carolina, Tennessee, Kentucky, Alabama, Mississippi, California and Texas.* Austin, TX, Arthur, Ben C. Jones & Co., 1901. 2, xvi, 327p. [L6339; D4611].

FOWLER -- Fowler, Grover Parsons. *The House of Fowler; A History of the Fowler Families of the South, Embracing Descendants of John Fowler of Virginia and Branches in North Carolina, Georgia, Tennessee, Kentucky, Alabama, Texas; Also Records of Allied Families.* Hickory, NC, 1940. 754, 2p. [L6343; VV].
-- *Index* by Mrs. Frank Cline, Hot Springs, AR, 1962. 69 l. [L6343].

FOX -- Adams, Nellie Fox and Bertha Fox Walton. *Fox Cousins By The Dozens.* Ashland, (FX shows as Ashton) KY, Economy Printers, 1976. vi l., 408p. [C237; X-FW/NY].

FOX -- Adams, Nellie Fox and Bertha Fox Walton. *Fox Cousins By The Dozens.*

Winchester, KY, Adams, San Pedro, CA, 1976. vi leaves, 408p. [D4624].

FRANCIS -- Katz, Gertrude Price. *David Rowland Francis (1850-1927) Member of the Price - Broaddus Families of Kentucky, and Wife Jane Perry... Other Allied Families, Wife Perry, Mother - Rowland and Caldwell.* Valley Stream, NY, 1972. 1 v. various pagings. [S906].

FRANCIS -- Katz, Gertrude Price. *Thomas Francis, Soldier in the War of 1812, and Wife, Polly Broaddus, and Their Thirteen Children; With a Military Record of Thomas Francis, d. 1813, 10th Regiment, Boswell's Kentucky Militia, Way of 1812 in Capt. John Duvall's Company of Infantry. 2d Draft.* NP, 1972. 8 leaves. [S907].

FRAME -- Feighny, R. R. *William and Susannah Frame of Pennsylvania, Virginia and Kentucky and Some of Their Descendants.* Topeka, KS, 196_. 77p. 2 leaves. [X-FW; VV].

FRASER -- Cox, Gloria M. *Descendants of George Frazier, Patrick Calvert, Thomas Endicott, Sr., John Ashworth, Sr. as They Entered "Into This Fruitful Valley" -Rev. ed. 1st ed. rev.* Owensboro, KY, Cook-McDowell Publications, 1980. v, 300, 15p. [C239].

FRYMAN -- Williams, Dudley C. *Phillip Fryman, Sr., Harrison County, Kentucky: Ancestors & Descendants.* Lexington, KY, D. C. Williams, 1986. 7, 103, 6 leaves. 1. Fryman family. 2. Fryman, Phillip-Family. 3. Kentucky- Genealogy. [G243].

FUGGER -- Fueger, Jean Haynes. *Our Heritage: Past, Present and Future. Fugger and Haynes Families.* Utica, KY, McDowell Publications, 1983. 472p. 2 leaves of plates. [C243; NG44].

FULENWIDER -- Bell, Raymond Martin. *The Vollenweider Family in America: Henry*

Fullenweider--Kentucky, Jacob Fullenweider (Fullewider)--Maryland, Jacob Ful(l)enweider--North Carolina, Ulrich Ful(len)weider--Virginia. Washington, PA, R. M. Bell, 1983. i, 25, 31 leaves. [C244; VV].

G

GAINES -- Collins, Anne C. [G248]. See above: COLLINS. [G150].

GAINES -- Gaines, Marietta G. *Marietta Gaines Memorandum Book.* Florence, KY, 1954. 25p. 5 leaves. D gives 25 leaves. [D4793; X-FW/CH].

GANTLEY -- Gantley, Anita Chinn. *Gantley and Related Lines.* Frankfort, KY, A. C. Gantley, 1982. 48 l. [C248].

GARDINER -- McPeak, Elizabeth B. *The Gardiner-Johnson Family. (Kentucky-Illinois).* Denver, CO, 19__, 29p. [X-DP].

GARNETT -- Garnett, James. *Judge James Garnett, 1834-1905. His Ancestors and Desceandants.* Louisville, KY, Author, 1934. 43p. [X-FW].

GARRARD -- des Cognets, Anna Russell. *Governor Garrard of Kentucky, His Descendants and Relatives.* Lexington, KY, J. M. Byrees, 1898. 1 v. 4, 134p. [L6670].

GARRARD -- des Cognets, Louis, Jr. *Governor Garrard of Kentucky, His Descendants and Relatives. And a Postscript About the Garrard Family.* Princeton, NJ, 1962. 279p. [L6671].

GARRED -- Garred, Ulysses Victoria. *A History and Genealogy of the Garreds, Jarretts of Kentucky and Many Related Families.* Whiting, IA, John Holmes Pub. Co., 1957. 321p. [D4864].

GARRETT -- Garrett, Hester Elizabeth. *A Book of Garretts: Supplement Number Two;*

Includes All Known Garretts not included in Supplement No. 1. Owensboro, KY, McDowell Publications, 1981. i, 166p. C also shows 4 pages of plates. [C250; NG; VV].

GARRETT -- Garrett, Hester Elizabeth. *A Book of Garretts: Supplement Number Three.* Owensboro, KY, McDowell Publications, 1983-1985. 2 v. Vol. 2: Supplement number three addenda. 1. Garrett family. 2. Garrett, Hester Elizabeth, 1903- Book of Garretts, 1600-1960. [G251].

GARRISON -- Power, Paul Edwin. *The Garrison and Allied Families.* Bowling Green, KY, P. E. Power, 1981. ii, 142p. [DS256].

GATLIFF -- Black, Helan J. *Gatliff Family, Ancestors and Descendants of Captain Charles Gatliff of Va. and Ky.* Wichita, KS, 1970. 122p. [X-FW; VV].

GATLIFF -- Gilbert, Dorothy [Louise]. *History of the Gatliff Family and Kin in the Southeastern United States of America: From Personal Papers of My Aunt Clara Gatliff Evans, My Mother Nolia Gatliff Gilbert, Both were Natives of Whitley County, Kentucky, Town of Williamsburg.* Alexandria, VA, D. Gilbert, 1984. 5, 11 leaves. [C252].

GAW -- Roper, Mary Louise Gaw. [G253]. See above: DE YOUNG. [G181].

GAYLORD -- Gaylord, Nancy Lou Allen. *The Pioneer Gaylord Family, 1630-1989: 359 Years in America.* Utica, KY, McDowell Publications, 1989. 172p. 1. Gaylord family. 2. Michigan-Genealogy. [G253].

GETTELFINGER -- Gettelfinger, F. J. *The Family Tree of Frederick Gettelfinger and Ursula Fessel.* New Haven, KY, Gettelfinger, 1967. 100p. [D4950].

GIBBS -- Gibbs, Vernon Lee. *The Gibbs Family History and Their Relatives of the Olden*

Times. Utica, KY, McDowell Publications, 1990. xiv, 179p. 1. Gibbs family. 2. Kentucky-Genealogy. [G257].

GIBBS -- Jenkins, Rella Gibbs. *Gibbs Family Record*. Utica, KY, McDowell Publications, 1983, 154p. [C256].

GILBERT -- Gilbert, Dorothy [Louise]. *The Gilberts of Southeastern United States*. Falls Church, VA, Gilbert, 1979. iv, 29, A-F leaves. [C257].

GILBERT -- Price, Mary F. *History of the Gilbert Family of Maryland, Virginia, Kentucky, et al.* NP, 1948. 71p. [X-FW; VV].

GILLILAND -- Elder, Ruth Estells Gilliland. *Transcribed Papers of the Settlement of the Estate Papers of Hiram Alexander Gilliland My Great Grandfather [for] John Marshall Chapter, Kentucky DAR, GRC*. NP, 1974. 80 l. [DC1422].

GILLIS -- Hester Cleo Gillis. *A History of the Gillis Family of Anderson County, Kentucky*. Lexington, KY, Hester, 1970. vi, 61 leaves. [D5008].

GILMORE -- Beanblossom, Walter S. *Gilmore Family Genealogy; "I Walk in the Light"; The Ancestors and Descendants of John Smith Gilmore*. Hawesville, KY, W.S. & F.F. Beanblossom, 1969. 143p. D omits emphasized portion of title. [D5017; X-FW].

GILMORE -- Thomas, Helen Gilmore Smith and Dolly Reed Gilmore Barman. *Gillmore - Carter and Allied Families*. Bowling Green, KY, 1962. 152p. [L6866].

GILPIN -- Perkins, George Gilpin. *The Kentucky Gilpins*. Washington, DC, Perkins, 1927. 129p. [L6872; D5024].

GODBOLD -- Shoemaker, Anne G. Golman. *The Godbold and Golman Connections - 1st ed. -*

Murray, KY, A. G. G. Shoemaker, 1987. 125p. 1. Godbold family. 2. Golman family. 3. Southern States-Genealogy. [G262].

GOFF -- Goff, Thomas Theodore. *Ancestors and Descendants of James Goff of Androscoggin, Maine, Isaac Goff of Utah, Elijah Goff of Hart and Green Counties, Kentucky, and Iowa.* Woodland Hills, CA, Bartels, 1976. iv, 128 l. [D5092].

GOLMON -- Shoemaker, Anne G. Golman. [G264]. See above: GODBOLD. [G262].

GOOD -- Goode, Cecil E. *Kentucky Cousins: The Goode Family of Barren County, Kentucky; The Ancestors and Posterity of Joseph Goode, 1833-1901.* NP, Goode, 1967. v, 201p. D lists under GOODE. [L6964; D5108].

GOOD -- Goode, Cecil E. *Kentucky Cousins: The Goode Family of Barren County, Kentucky, and Related Families: Accounts of Goode, Anderson, Baker, Cary, Combs, Cozzart, Jones, Mulky, Sherfey, Starr, White, and Wren Families. 2nd ed. rev ed.* Glasgow, KY, C. E. Goode, 1982. vi, 249p. [C265].

GOODBAR -- Clark, Carmen E. *Goodbars I Found, 1774-1978: Descendants of Joseph (1) and William (2) of Rockbridge.* Lexington, KY, 1980. [VV].

GOODE -- Goode, Cecil E. *Kentucky Cousins.* Glasgow, KY, Goode, 1982. vi, 249p. [DS277].

GOODE -- Williams, Deward C. *The Pedigree of the Goode Family From the Emperor Charlemagne to the Allied Families of Coffey and White of Kentucky, Indiana and Illinois.* Mt. Carmel, IL, Williams, 1977. 14p. [D5110].

GOODPASTURE -- Goodpasture, Robert Abraham. *Early Goodpaster (Goodpasture) Families in America.* Sunnyvale, CA, 1972. 1 v. 5 parts. Pt. 1. Virginia, Tennessee, Kentucky, Ohio 1st ed; rev. - Pt. 2 Kentucky, Ohio, Indiana, Illinois, Iowa Records. [S1022].

GOTT -- Cook, Rohease Brown. *A Record of the Descendants of John Gott of Maryland, Logan Co., Ky., & White Co., Ill. and of His Son-in-Law, James E. Wrenwick of South Carolina and White County, Ill.* Erie, PA, Cook, 1965. 146, 2p. D shows 145 leaves. [D5169; X-FW/PH].

GOULD -- Gold, Delbert. *The Life Story of Washington Gold, 2nd ed.* NP, KY, D. Gold, 1983. x, 30 l. [C269].

GOVER -- Gover, Rose and Bess. *Gover, Immigrant to Maryland Colony in 1750: Biographical and Genealogical Sketches of the Descendants of John Gover (1731-1790) and Elizabeth Duvall (1738-1799).* Phoenix, AZ, R. Gover, Nancy, KY, B. Gover, 1982. Leaves A-J, xiv, 181p. [C270].

GRAHAM -- Barr, Lockwood. *...Graham Family of Virginia and Kentucky; Descendants of Christopher Graham Born in Scotland or Ireland, Who Settled First in Pennsylvania; and then Migrated to Virginia with His Family Before 1740.* Pelham Manor, NY, 1941. 20 leaves, [X-NY; VV].

GRAHAM -- Barr, Lockwood. *Genealogical Charts and Biographical Notes upon the Graham Familiy, Virginia and Kentucky.* Pelham Manor, NY, 1946. 1 vol. [X-NY].

GRAHAM -- Millis, Mary Ruth. *A Graham Chronicle: Records of the Craig and Graham Families, and Including Kintners of Indiana, Hunts of Kentucky.* Dallas, TX, Millis, 1977. xiii, 488p. [C271].

GRANT -- Heller, Dick D. *Grant Family of Fauquier County, Va., Fleming County, Ky., Rush, Wabash, and Jasper Counties, Ind. in the 18th, 19th, and 20th Century.* Decatur, IN, 1974. [VV].

GRATZ -- Long, Jerry. *The Roots of Mabel Josephine Gratzer Long.* Owensboro, KY, McDowell Publications, 1980. 62 l. [C272].

GRAVES -- Clark, Sara Graves. *Some Lines of the Graves Family in the Blue Grass Region of Kentucky and Their Connections.* NP, 1963. 54 leaves. [D5223].

GRAVES -- Nacke, Judy. [G270]. See above. COX. [G162].

GREEN -- Dade, Thomas Green. *The Green Family of Virginia and Kentucky.* NP, 1969. 1 v. (various foliations). [D5251; VV].

GREENLEE -- Greenlee, Ralph S. *Genealogy of the Greenlee Families in America, Scotland, Ireland and England... Also Genealogical Data on the McDowells of Virginia and Kentucky.* Chicago, IL, Priv. Print., 1908. 744p., 115 plates. [X-LI/NY/PH; VV].

GRIFFITH -- Griffith, Anna Laura. *The Griffiths of Wales and America.* Mayfield, KY, Griffith, 1979. xi, 276, 38p. [C277].

GRIFFITH -- Griffiths, George R. *Robert Griffith From Carno, Wales And His Descendants.* Murray, KY, Lorrah & Hitchcock Publications, 1981. ii, 128p. [C277; NG48].

GRIMWOOD -- Grimwood, James Maurice. *Grimwood Sketches, 1562-1982.* Utica, KY, McDowell Publications, 1982. 253p. [DS287].

GROVER -- Grover, Charles. *Grovers: The Only Direct Line for James Luther Brumfield... Gallia County, Ohio.* Research by Marcia Conrad Brumfield. Maysfield, KY, Brumfield, 1990. 8 l. [DC1521]

GROVER -- Grover, Martha A. *A Genealogical History of the Descendants of Benoni Grover.* Lexington, KY, 1904. 46p. [X-LA].

GRUBB -- Grubbs, W. L. *The Grubbs Family in the United States and Particularly in Kentucky* *with Special Reference to My Own Branch of the Family*. Louisville, KY, Grubbs, 1971. vii, 107p. [S1071; D5355].

GULLETT -- Van Hoose, John See. [G280]. See above: BOONE. [G69].

GUPTON -- Shipp, Annis Gupton & Beard, Georgia Gupton. *The Guptons and Related Families*. Campbellsville, KY, Central Ky, News Journal, 1975. 48p. [DC1538].

GUTHRIE -- Guthrie, Joseph A. *Early Virginia Guthries and Their Kentucky Descendants*. Kansas City, MO, Guthrie, 1946. ix, 96p. [D5394; X-FW/MH; VV].

H

HADDON -- Brevoort, Eliza Haddon McClure. *History & Family Trees of Haddon & McClure Families - Virginia, Kentucky, Indiana*. NP, 1948. 187 l. [D5404].

HAGAN -- Hagan, Joseph G. *A Collection of Memories*. Utica, KY, McDowell Publications, 1982. 253p. 1. Hagan, Joseph G.-Family. 2. Hagan family. 3. Kentucky-Biography. 4. Kentucky-Genealogy. 5. Pullen family. 6. Alabama-Genealogy. [G288].

HAGAN -- Hamilton, Anna L. *The Genealogy of Thomas Clarke Hagan Family, 1793-1983: Irish Ancestors, Maryland Immigrant, Kentucky Pioneers, and Early American Catholic Heritage*. Whitesville, KY, Hamilton, 1985. 253p. 1. Hagan family. 2. Hagan, Thomas Clarke, 1793-1875. [G288; DC1549].

HAGAN -- Headrick, Marcella Pickerel. *Scattered Chips from the Woodpile*. Utica, KY, McDowell Publications, 1982. 70p. 1. Stroud family. 2. Hagan family. 3. Kentucky-Genealogy. [G288].

HALCOMB -- Giulvezan, Isabel Stebbins. *Notes on Hiram H. Halcomb (1789-1869) of*

Caswell County, North Carolina, Robertson County, Tennessee, Logan and Simpson Counties, Kentucky and His 16 Children. St. Louis, MO, Giulvezan, 1961. 55 l. FW gives no date. [D5436; X-FW].

HALE -- Crowe, Maude. *Descendants From First Familiesof Virginia and Maryland: A Family History and Genealogy Covering 350 Years, 1620-1970.* Fordsville, KY, M. Crowe, 1978. 228p. [C287].

HALL -- Akers, Carmel L. *The Halls of Muddy Creek.* Grethel, KY, Mud Creek Heritage Publishers, 1987. 2 v. (viii, 2009, 30p.) 1. Hall family. 2. Kentucky-Genealogy. [G290].

HALL -- Parrish, Verle Hamilton and Efonda S. Doughton. *Who's Who in My Hall Family (of Virginia, North Carolins (sic) and Kentucky).* Georgetown, KY, Verle H. Parrish, Farmington, UT, E. S. Daughton, 1982. 128P. [C289; VV].

HALL -- Williams, Dudley C. *Lee Roy Hall, 1846-1885, Fayette County, Kentucky: Ancestors and Descendants.* Lexington, KY, D. C. Williams, 1986. 5, 112 leaves. 1. Hall family. 2. Hall, Lee Roy, 1846-1887(?)-family. 3. Fayette County (Ky.)-Genealogy. [G290].

HAMILTON -- Hamilton, Anna L. *The Genealogy of Benjamin Thomas Hamilton, His Ancestors, Relatives, and Descendants.* Utica, KY, McDowell Publications, Whiteville, KY, Hamilton, 1988. 132p. 1. Hamilton family. 2. Hamilton, Benjamin Thomas, 1881-1963-Family. [G291; DC1574].

HAMILTON -- Parrish, Verle Hamilton. *Hamilton, Mullins, Fleming, and Related Families of Ky., W. Va., No. Car., Tenn.* Stamping Ground, KY, Parrish, 1975. 80p. [S1100].

HAMLIN -- Hamblin, Willard M. *Hamblin Family Reunion, Nevisdale, Whitley County, Kentucky, August 19, 1973. History of the*

Hamblin Family. Lexington, KY, 1973. 11p. [S1102].

HAMMAN -- Conner, Henry Clay. *The Life and Times of Philip Hamman.* Indianapolis, IN, Conner, 1982. 18, 220, 9p. Includes 1981 Supplement - Deeds to Property Owned by Philip Hamman in Montgomery Co., Kentucky., 1803-1823. [DS304].

HAMMER -- Hammers, Marian G. *The Hammers of Butler County, Kentucky.* Madisonville, KY, M. G. Hammers, 1982. 88, xxi p., 4 leaves of plates. [C292].

HAMMON -- Hammon, Stratton Owen. *The Sage of John Hammon, Revolutionary War Hero and Owen County, Kentucky Pioneer.* Louisville, KY, Author, 1979. 34, iv p. [DC1581].

HAMPTON -- NAS. *Hampton Family of Virginia, North and South Carolina & Kentucky.* NP, n.d. Pages not shown. [X-SL; VV].

HAMPTON -- Doan, John Hampton. *Hampton Family History; An Account of the Pennsylvania Hamptons in America in the Line of John Hampton, jr., of Wrightstown; with an Appendix Treating of Some Branches.* Milton, KY, Solomon E. Hampton, 1911. 199, 7p. [L7666; D5530].

HANCOCK -- Bloore, Helen L. *A Genealogical Record of the Descendants of Hancock - Cofer - Jones - Masssie Families of Virginia and Kentucky.* Glendale, CA, Bloor, 1962. 52p. [NG49; D5540].

HANKS -- Baber, Adin (with a number of Hank descendants). *The Hanks Family of Virginia and Westward; A Genealogical Record from the Early 1600's, Including Charts of Families in Arkansas, the Carolinas Georgia, Illinois, Indiana, Iowa, Kentucky, Missouri, Oklahama, Ohio, Pennsylvania, and Texas.* Kansas, IL, 1965. Sold exclusively by A. H Clark Co., Glendale, CA. 1 v. (various pagings). [L7685; VP; VV].

HANKS -- Baber, Adin. *The Hanks Family of Virginia and Westward; A Genealogical Record from the Early 1600's, Including Charts of Families in Arkansas, the Carolinas Georgia, Illinois, Indiana, Iowa, Kentucky, Missouri, Oklahama, Ohio, Pennsylvania, and Texas.* A. H. Clarke & Co., Glendale, CA, 1965. [VP].

HARDIN -- Hardin, Jack R. *History of the Hardin Family in the Early Settling of Kentucky.* Louisville, KY, Baptist World Publ. Co., 1915. 272p. X libraries show 116p. [D5588; X-DP/SW/SP].

HARDIN -- Huron, Frances Harding. *Some Hardin, Harding and Related Families of Virginia, Pennsylvania, Kentucky and Indiana.* Winchester, VA, F. H. Huron, 1987. 113 leaves. [DC1614].

HARDIN -- Wulfeck, Dorothy Ford. *Hardin and Harding of Virginia and Kentucky.* Naugatuck, CT, Wulfeck, 1963. 126p. [S1120].

HARDIN -- Wulfeck, Dorothy Ford. *Supplement to Hardin and Harding (of Virginia and Kentucky), Naugatuck, CT, (1963) Supplement (sic).* Naugatuck, CT, D. F. Wulfeck, 1965. 41p. [X-FW/NY].

HARDIN -- Wulfeck, Dorothy Ford. *Hardin and Harding of Virginia and Kentucky and Supplement.* Naugatuck, CT, Wulfeck, 1963-65. 2 v. in 1. [D5594].

HARNED -- McClure, Dorothy Welch and Lorenza D. Carby. *Family of John Harned and Elizabeth A. Duncan of Breckenridge Co., Kentucky.* Yucaipa, CA, R. W. Fentress, 1984. 100, 46 leaves. 1. Harned family. 2. Harned, John, 1805-1881-Family. 3. Duncan, Elizabeth A., 1805-1854-Family. 4. Breckenridge County (Ky.)-Genealogy. [G299; C298].

HARPER -- Harris, Fanchon Harper; Stokes. Nancy Harris, & Taylor, Lois Harris. *Harper - Clark Family Graves County, Kentucky.* NP, 1985. 37p. [DC1629].

HARPER -- Ward, Myrtle Harper and Wanda Ward Bullock. *The Harpers: The Descendants of Silas and Elizabeth Harper.* Pulaski County, KY, 162p. [C299].

HARRELL -- Carby, Delbert Mrs. *The Noah Harrell Family of Grayson Co., Kentucky.* Clarkson KY, D. Carby, 1978. 146 l. C gives 148 leaves. 1. Harrell family. 2. Harrel, Noah, 1776-1805-Family. 3. Grayson County (Ky.)-Genealogy. [G300; C299].

HARRELL -- Carby, Lorenza Duncan. *The Richard and Winifred Compton Harrell Family of Breckenridge and Grayson Cos., Kentucky. Information from the Descendants Who Lived in the Duff and Pilgrim Communities.* Yucaipa, CA, R. W. Fentress, 1980. a-b, 60 l. [C299].

HARRIS -- Seaman, Catherine Hawes Coleman. [G301]. See above: COLEMAN. [G150].

HARRIS -- Johnston, William Preston. *Edward Harris and His Ancestors 1634-1820.* Louisville, KY, J. P. Morton & Company, 1899. 26p. [L7810].

HARRISON -- Johnson, Leona Grace Ellis. *Harrisons of Virginia, Kentucky and Indiana: Genealogy of John, Thomas, and Their Sister Nancy Pell, Their Descendants and Some Allied Lines.* New Richmond, WI, Johnson, 1988. 448p. 1. Harrison family. 2. Virginia-Genealogy. 3. Harrison, John, 1771-1862, 4. Kentucky-Genealogy. 5. Indiana-Genealogy. [G302; DC1654].

HART -- Wilson, Samuel Mackay. *Susan Hart Shelby; A Memoir by S.M.W. (Samuel Mackay Wilson).* Lexington, KY, 1923. 66p. [L7879].

HATFIELD -- Hatfield, G. Elliott. *(The) Hatfields. Rev. and ed. by Leonard Roberts.* Stanville, KY, Big Sandy Valley Historical Soc., 1974. 207p. Charts of W. Va., Ky. Hatfields. [X-FW/SL].

HATFIELD -- Hatfield, G. Elliott. *(The) Hatfields. Rev. and ed. by Leonard Roberts and Henry P. Scalf - Rev. ed.* Stanville, KY, Big Sandy Valley Hisotrical Soc., 1988. xi, 329p., 24p. of plates. 1. Hatfield - McCoy Feud. 2. Hatfield family. [G304].

HAWES -- Hudgins, Helen Hawes. *The Richard Hawes Family of Kentucky.* Franklin, KY, H. H. Hudgins, 1986. iv, 27p. [DC1685].

HAWKINS -- Claypool, E. A., Genealogist. *Hawkins Records: South Carolina, North Carolina, Delaware, Kentucky.* NP, 1902. 124p. 9 leaves. [X-FW].

HAWKINS -- Gladden, Sanford Charles. *Descendants of Stephen C. Hawkins of Campbell County, Kentucky; Allied Families of Barton, Clephane, Eckert, Marshall, & Thomasson.* Boulder, CO, Gladden, 1965. 160p. [L8016; NG51; D5826].

HAWKINS -- James, Jessamine Bland. *Some Kentucky Court Records of the Hawkins and Bourn Families.* NP, 1973. xviii, 28 l. [D5832].

HAWKINS -- Singer, J. W. *Hawkins-Jesse Family.* Stamping Ground, KY, 1972. 47p. [X-FW].

HAWKINS -- Wulfeck, Dorothy Ford. *Hawkins of Virginia, the Carolinas and Kentucky; Court Records, Queries, Brief Lineages, Genealogical Notes.* Naugutuck, CT, 1962. 86p. D shows 86 leaves and date of 1963. [D5834; X-SU; VV].

HAYES -- Repass, Mary Eva Berry. *The Hayes Family of Lawrence County, Kentucky: Descendants of Bazeal Hayes.* Fredericksburg, VA, 1978. [VV].

HAYES -- Seaman, Catherine Hawes Coleman. [G307]. See above: COLEMAN. [G150].

HAYES -- Walter, Lora Thelma Chandler and Theodore B. Walter. *A Genealogical Record of* *the Descendants of Bazeal Hayes of Charley, Lawrence County, Kentucky.* Baltimore, MD, Gateway Press, 1981. ix, 980p. 1 leaf of plates. [C307; NG51].

HAYNER -- Rosenagle, Laura Elva. *The John and Jane Fleming Hayes Family Genealogy. -- 1st ed.* Utica, KY, McDowell Publications, 1983. xvi, 486p. [C307].

HAYS -- Litsey, David R. *Hays Family in Kentucky and Their Descendants.* Springfield, KY, 1949. Unpaged. [X-FW].

HEAD -- Head, Henry Everett. *My Head Family in Kentucke (sic).* __, Kentucky, H. E. Head, 1981. vi, 234 l. [C308].

HEADINGTON -- McDonald, David George. *Zebulon Headington: A Brief History of the Life and Descendants of Zebulon Headington of Baltimore County, Maryland and Harrison County, Kentucky.* Columbia, MO, D. G. McDonald, 1983. 1 v. various pagings. [C308].

HECK -- Heck, Earl Leon Werley. *The History of the Heck Family of America, with Special Attention to Those Families Who Originated in Indiana, Kentucky, Maryland, Ohio, Pennsylvania and Virginia.* Englewood, OH, Heck, 1959. 50p. [L8136; D5910].

HEINER -- Hensell, John. *Chronicles of a German Family; or Heiners of Germany, Pennsylvania, Kentucky and Texas.* Houston, TX, J. Hensell, 1958. [VP].

HEIZER -- Heizer, James Marion. *The Heizer Family.* Louisville, KY, Heizer, 1969. 180, 20p. [D5925].

HELBERG -- Helberg, Barbara K. *Helberg Family History.* Utica, KY, McDowell Publications, 1987. vii, 196p. 1. Helberg family. 2. Germany-Genealogy. 3. Ohio-Genealogy. [G310].

HELM -- Hoffman, Glady Stutler. *Helm - DeMar and Some Allied Pioneer Families of Kentucky.* Atlanta, GA, G. S. Hoffmann, 1973. 97 leaves. D shows NP & no publisher. [D5931; DC1721].

HENDERSON -- NAS. *Henderson Research - Virginia, Georgia, Ky., Tenn.* Cincinnati, OH, NP, n.d. [VV].

HENDERSON -- Henderson, Alvena Wells. *Henderson Ancestors and Descendants.* Eubank, KY, A. W. Henderson and E. H. Fisher, 1989. 4, iii, 425p. 1. Henderson family. 2. Kentucky-Genealogy. [G311].

HENDERSON -- Lloyd, Emma Rouse. *The Henderson Family of Pennsylvania and Kentucky.* (Available for Consultation at Lloyd Library, 309 West Court Street, Cincinnati, OH.) NP, n.d., no pagination. [L8194; VP].

HENDERSON -- Roberts, H. D. *Henderson Family Research; (Virginia, Kentucky, Tennessee, Georgia, Indiana, etc.)* Orange, CA, Author, 1967. 15p. [X-FW; VV].

HENDRICKS -- Hendricks Fam. Org. Res. Staff. *Abraham Hendricks and Family. - The Kentucky-Missouri Epoch.* NP, n.d. Pages not given. [X-IG].

HENDRICKS -- Moeller, Josephine F. *George Hendricks, Illinois Pioneer and His Descendants.* Utica, KY, McDowell Publications, 1982. 196p. [DS335].

HENKEL -- Riley, Jean M. Hinkle . *A History and Genealogy of the Henckle's and/or Hinkle's from the Sixteenth Century in Germany to the Twentieth Century in the United States of America.* Paducah, KY, J.M.H. Riley, 1988. 61, A-U p., 2 leaves of plates. 1. Henkel family. 2. Hinkle family. 3. Germany-Genealogy. 4. Kentucky-Genealogy. [G312].

HENRY -- Henry, John Flournoy. *A History of the Henry Family From Its Beginning in this*

Country to the Present Time. Louisville, KY, John P. Morton & Co., 1900. ix, 125p. [L8201; DC1738].

HENRY -- Henry, John Flournoy. *A History of the Henry Family.* Louisville, KY, John P. Morton & Co., 1926. 125p. [D5974].

HERNDON -- Taylor, Edwin J., Jr. *A Kentucky Lady; A Short Biography of Catherine Herndon Sterrett. Also Washington, Taylor, Throckmorton Families.* Bismarck, ND, 1966. 45p. [NG52].

HESS -- Barekman, June B. & Elsie R. Swartz. *Who is William Hess? A Sketch of the Family of Appolos Hess WhoCame to Shelby County, Kentucky, before 1819 to Floyd and Clark Counties, Indiana. Being the Lineage of, as far as possible of (sic) one Son, William Hess Whose Later Kin are Found in Washington and Knox Counties, Indiana.* Chicago, IL, Hoosier Gals Press, 1971. 20 leaves. [S1190].

HESTER -- Searl, Hester Geraldine Lester. *History and Genealogy; A Story of Some Descendants of John Hester, an Early Settler of Fleming County, Kentucky, Who Arrived in America in the Year 1740. Also Included is Genealogy of many Collateral Families.* Patterson, CA, 1972. xii, 492p. [S1191].

HICKMAN -- Hickman, Clarence N. *Genealogy of the Hickman Families of Virginia, Kentucky, Indiana, and Texas.* Jackson Heights, NY, 1967. 83p. [L8316; VV].

HICKMAN -- Hilton, Hope A. *Edwin and Elender Webber Childs Hickman; Some Progenitors and Descendants, Early Pioneers of Virginia, North Carolina, Kentucky, Missouri, and Utah.* Salt Lake City, UT, 1967. iv, 151p. [L8315; VV].

HIGGINS -- Powell, Omegene Powers. [G317]. See above. BASHAM. [G38].

HIGGS -- Higgs, Charles Leonard. *Genealogy, The Higgs Family in the area of Trivoli, Peoria County, State of Illinois.* Owensboro, KY, Westerfield Print. Co., 1974. 68 leaves. [S1201].

HILL -- Hill, John David. *Thomas Hill and Descendants.* Louisville, KY, John P. Morton & Co., 1900. vi, 200p. [L8368; D6105].

HILL -- Hill, Lillard. Henry. *Genealogy of the Hill Family of Garrard and Madison Counties, Kentucky.* NP, Hill, New York, NY, Unigraphic, Inc., 1978. iv, 279 leaves. [C321; D6107].

HILL -- Young, David Gordon. *Genealogy of the Hill Family, Kentucky and Virginia.* NP, Francis Hill Kuhn, 1969. 75p. SU shows 1 vol. Variously paged. [D6116; X-SU; VV].

HILLIARD -- Hilliard, Gena Finch. *The Bartlett Hilliard Family, Ancestors and Descendants.* Clinton, KY, Hilliard, 1973. 85p. [S1210; D6120].

HILLIGOSS -- Danell, Jennie. *Hilligoss Family Fleming County, Ky. and Rush County, Indiana.* Fresno, CA, n.d. Pages not given. [X-FW].

HILLIGOSS -- Hilligoss, Lillie A. *Hilligoss Family of Pennsylvania, Fleming County, Ky., and Rush County, Ind.* NP, 1901. 28p. [X-FW; VP].

HINDS -- NAS. *Hines and Allied Families of Virginia and Kentucky.* NP, 1911. Geneal. Table. [L8417].

HINES -- Hines, James Davis. *Descendants of Henry Hines, sr., 1732-1810.* Louisville, KY, J. P. Morton & Company, 1925. 2, 35p. [L8421].

HINKLE -- Riley,Jean M. Hinkle. [G320]. See above: HENKEL. [G312].

HOBBS -- Lewis, Ailine F. *The Hobbs: Jacob Henry... Millard F. and Allied Lines from N.C., Va., Ky. 1764-1987.* NP, Missouri, DAR 1987. 105 l. [DC1798].

HODGES -- Taylor, Mary Evelena. *Apples of the Tree of S. Agnes Hodges: A Family Genealogy - 1st ed.* Louisville, KY, M. E. Taylor, 1983. ix, 126p. [C325].

HOLLINGSWORTH -- Stewart, J. Adger. *Descendants of Valentine Hollingsworth, Sr.* Louisville, KY, John P. Morton & Co., 1925. 3, 208p. Based on the "Hollingsworth Genealogy Memorandum... by William B. Hollingsworth... 1884", with additions and corrections. [L8539; D6234].

HOLLEY -- Day, William Henry. *A Genealogical History of the Holley Family and Waters Family.* Danville, IN, W.H. Day and S.J. Holley, Utica, KY, McDowell Publications, li, 815p., 1. Holley family. 2. Waters family. [G327].

HOLLON -- Hollon, Clay. *Genealogy of Hollon and Related Families, Eastern Ky.* Chicago, IL, 1958. 108p. [NG53].

HOLMES -- Joiner, Ransey. *Holmes - Bradley, A History of Our Ancestors.* Mayfield, KY, 1973. 34p. [NG53; X-FW].

HOLMES -- Nash, James Henry. *The Homeplace: The Ancestors and Descendants of Edward Walker Nash and Louisa Mentoria Holmes.* Mayfield, KY, J.H. Nash, 1989. iv, 139p. 1. Nash family. 2. Holmes family. 3. Nash, Edward Walker, 1833-1914-Family. 4. Holmes, Louisa Mentoria, 1840-1928-Family. 5. Georgia-Genealogy. [G327].

HOPKINS -- NAS. *Ezekiel and Sarah Hazzard Hopkins of... Bourbon County, Kentucky... Including Related Families.* NP, Williamsburg Virginia Chapter, DAR, 1978. 1 v. in various foliations. [DC1843].

HOPKINS -- Ball, Helen A. *Ezekiel and Sarah Hazzard Hopkins of Delaware, Maryland, Pennsylvania and Bourbon County, Kentucky Including Some of Their Descendants and Related Families.* East Lansing, MI, H. A. Ball, 1978. 150p. [C332].

HOPKINS -- Ball, Helen A., editor. *Ezekiel and Sarah Hazzard Hopkins of Delaware, Maryland, Pennsylvania and Bourbon County, Kentucky.* East Lansing, MI, H. A. Ball, 1978. ca 400p. [DC1841; VP].

HOPKINS -- Ball, Helen A. *Ezekiel and Sarah Hazzard Hopkins of Delaware, Maryland, Pennsylvania and Bourbon County, Kentucky Including Some of Their Descendants. 2nd ed.* East Lansing, MI, H. A. Ball, 1980. 1 v. various pagings. [VP].

HOPKINS -- Bruhn, Reva Hopkins. *Hopkins Forever: James Hopkins, Revolutionary Soldier, Virginia, North Carolina, Kentucky, Tennessee, Illinois, and Missouri.* Visalia, CA, R. H. Bruhn, 1984. ii, 74p. 110 pages of plates. [C332; VV].

HOPPER -- Hopper, Roselea. *Hopper Hunters.* Burkburnett, TX, S. and J. Parks, 1980 (1985 printing). 40, ix leaves. "A compilation of all Hopper information researched and printed by Roselea Greer Hopperfrom Records of Missouri, Illinois, Kentucky, and Virginia, plus letters and information from other Hopper researchers and appendix 1985". 1. Hopper family. 2. Missouri-Genealogy. 3. Kentucky-Genalogy. [G330].

HORLACHER -- Horlacher, Levi Jackson & Vaneta T. *Family of Hans Michael and Maria Veronica Horlacher.* Lexington, KY, 1968. 326p. [NG54].

HORLACHER -- Horlacher, Levi Jackson & Vaneta T. *Family of Hans Michael and Maria Veronica Horlacher. 2nd ed.* Lexington, KY, Horlacher, Horlacher, 1974. 100 l. D gives 106 leaves. [S1244; D6323].

HORNING -- Leslie, E. Glen. [G330]. See above: FORD. [G235].

HOUGH -- Hough, James Emerson. *Kentucky Heritage: The Lineage of William Hough and His Descendants.* Bardstown, KY, Hough, 1978. vi, 109p. [C334].

HOUSTON -- Campbell, Leslie L. *The Houston Family of Virginia.* Lexington, KY, 1956. [VV].

HOVERMALE -- Roach, Charles W. *The Hovermales of Morgan Co., W. Va., Bath Co., Ky., Washington Co., Md.* Parkland, WA, C. W. Roach, Jr., 1986. 116 leaves. 1. Hovermale family. 2. Morgan County (W.Va.)-Genealogy. 3. Bath County (Ky.)-Genealogy. 4. Washington County (Md.)-Genealogy. [G333].

HOWARD -- Dunham, Frances Yeager. *Howards in Southeastern Kentucky. Limited ed.* Pensacola, FL, Dunham, 1979. viii, 334p., 1 leaf of plates. [C336].

HOWARD -- Hamilton, Anna L. *The Genealogy of the Howards of Daviess County, Kentucky and Their Ancestors: English Ancestors, Maryland Emigrants, Kentucky Pioneers, and Early American Catholic Heritage.* Utica, KY, McDowell Publications. 1984. 220, 43p., 26 p. of plates. 1. Howard family. 2. Daviess County (Ky.)-Genealogy. [G333].

HOWARD -- Hamilton, Anna L. *The Genealogy of the Howards of Daviess County, Kentucky and Their Ancestors.* Whiteville, KY, Hamilton, 1984. 304p. [DC1867].

HOWE -- Whitley, Olga Rolater. *The Howe Line, Pennsylvania, South Carolina, Kentucky; With Connections, Dunlap, McKenzie, Patrick, and Biggers.* Commerce, TX, 1967. [VP].

HUBBARD -- Bowling, Noland. [G335]. See above: BARTON. [G38].

HUBBARD -- Bowling, Noland. *Meet Your Ancestors: Some Descendants of Robert Hubbard (ca. 1600-1663) Westmoreland, New Kent, Amelia, Halifax, Lunenburg, Pittsylvania Counties, Virginia and Other States: Families Allied by Marriage, Arnn (Aron, Aaron), Adkins, (Atkins), Clement (Clements), Fuller, Giles, Gilbert, Harris, Linthicum, Mitchell, and Pigg.* Utica, KY, McDowell, Publications, 1985. 618, lxxxvi, xxxvi p. of plates. 1. Hubbard family. 2. Hubbard, Robert, ca. 1600- ca. 1663 3. Virginia-Genealogy. [G335].

HUDIBURGH -- Roper, Mary Louise Gaw. [G335]. See above: DE YOUNG. [G181].

HUDSON -- Harrison, Sallie Stewart. *Hutson Family.* Utica, KY, McDowell Publications, 198_. ii, 244p. 1. Hudson family. 2. Texas-Genealogy. [G335].

HUGHES -- Hughes, Lydia Annie and Richard Hughes Sullivan. *Hughes Family of Kentucky and Virginia.* Columbia, SC, 1920. 48p. Previously published in 1902. [L8858; X-FW; VV].

HUGHES -- Hughes, W. J. L. *The Hughes Family and Connections, Especially the Gass, Ward and Boze Families.* Owensboro, KY, Hughes, 1911. xvii, 19-164p. [L8854; D6499].

HUNT -- Brown, Mrs. Herbet (Imogene Hannan Brown). *Hunt - Denton Families of Va., Tenn., Ky., Ind., and Western States.* Alexandria, IN, 1969. 719 l. [S1286; VV].

HUNT -- Rowland, Elaine. *William Hunt and Sarah Mills: Their Ancestors and Ours: Essays and Genealogies.* Owensboro, KY, McDowell Publications, 1981. xii, 162p. [C342].

HUNTER -- James, Jessamine B. *Hunter and Alford Families of Virginia and Kentucky.* Tucson, AZ, James, 1954. 50 leaves. [D6564; VV].

HURST -- Hurst, J.C. *(Hursts of Shenandoah:) Also Keyser, Landsaw.* Lexington, KY, Hurst, 198_. 175p. DS title in ( ) above. [DC1928; DS378].

HURT -- Blevins, Ray E. *Hurts from South Carolina to Wayne County, Kentucky.* Johnson City, TN, Overmountain Press, 1989. 216p. 1. Hurt family. 2. South Carolina-Genealogy. 3. Kentucky-Genealogy. [G339].

HUTCHERSON -- Campbell, Kathryn Hutcherson. *That Kentucky Hutcherson.* NP, Campbell, 1970. 87 leaves. [D6599].

HUTCHINSON -- Wilson, Wesley G. *Norristown Folks.* Utica, KY, McDowell Publications, 1988- v. <1 >. Bibliography v. 1, p. 255-256. 1. Hutchinson family. 2. Hutcheson, John, 1767-1836-Family. 3. Norristown (Ga.)-Genealogy. 4. Georgia-Genealogy. [G340].

HUTZEL -- Hutsell, Sue and Jane Hutsell Terral. *Our Hutzell - Hutsell Family.* Covington, KY, O. S. Hutsell, 1980. vii, 780p., 73 leaves of plates. [C344].

I

INGLES -- Maes, Virginia Ingles. *The Descendants of Bartlett Haley Ingles and Margaret Allison of Pennsylvania, Kentucky, and Illinois, with Data on the Direct Descendants and on the Collateral Lines of Bevan, Boone, DeHart, Haley, Harmer, Richardson.* Rushville, IL, 1940. 27 leaves. [L9086].

IRVIN -- Morris, Margaret Logan. *The Irvins, Doaks, Logans, and McCampbells of Virginia and Kentucky.* Corydon, IN, 1916. [VV].

IRVINE -- Boyd, Mrs. Lucinda. *The Irvines and Their Kin.* Louisville, KY, Boyd, 1898. 115p. [L9114; D6678].

IRVINE -- Sea, Sophia Fox. *The Irvines of Madison County, Kentucky.* Register of Kentucky State Historical Society, v. 3, no. 8, May, 1905. [NG56].

IRVINS -- Morris, Margaret Logan. *The Irvins, Doaks, Logans, and McCampbells of Virginia and Kentucky.* Indianapolis, IN, C. E. Pauley & Co., 1916. [VV].

J

JACKSON -- Gerlach, Mary Ruth Jackson. *Isaac Jackson, Virginia, 1797 Bullitt County, Kentucky, 1822 and Descendants.* Louisville, KY, M. R. J. Gerlach, 1985. 983p. [C350].

JACKSON -- Gross, Dorothy P. *Christopher Maccabeus Jackson of Virginia and Kentucky, ca. 1737-1804.* Edmonds, WA, Gross, 1990. 1 v. in various paginations. [DC1968].

JACKSON -- Jackson, Harry L. *Some Descendants of John and Elizabeth Cummins Jackson in Kentucky: Kentucky Relatives of Stonewall Jackson.* Cleveland, OH, Jackson, (X shows Clarksville, TN, Jostens Publications), 1976. 154p. [C350; D6703; X-FW/LA/OH].

JACKSON -- Jackson, William Neel. *Jacksons of Kentucky, Their Ancestors and Descendants.* Bowling Green, KY, 1982. 401p. [NG56].

JACKSON -- Jackson, William Neel. *Jacksons of Kentucky, Their Ancestors and Descendants.* Owensboro, KY, McDowell, 1982. 374p., 1 leaf of plates. [C350].

JACKSON -- Shoop, Michael I. *The Genealogies of the Jackson, Junkin and Morris on Families.* Lexington, KY,Garland Gray Memorial Research Center, Stonewall Jackson House, Historic Lexington Foundation, 1981. [VV].

JAMES -- Burke, Gary C. *James - Ward Family of Kentucky.* Los Angeles, CA, 1936. 65p. [X-LA].

JAMES -- Hobbs, Dorcas M. *James Family.* Pikeville, KY, 1972. 7p. [X-FW].

JAMES -- Scalf, Henry Preston. *Mountain Kinsmen Ride; A Story of the James Family.* Prestonburg, KY, 1956. 11p. [L9195].

JARRETT -- Garred, Ulysses Victoria. *History and Genealogy of the Garrads, Jarretts of Kentucky and Many Related Families.* Whiting, IA, J. Holmes, Pub. Co., 1957. 321p. [L9214].

JENKINS -- Jenkins, Rella Gibbs. *Family Record of Bartholomew and Nancy Baker Jenkins and Joe and Sarah Gill King.* Madisonville, KY, R. G. Jenkins, 1983. 42 leaves. 1. Jenkins family. 2. King family. 3. Jenkins, Bartholomew, ca. 1797-1863-Family. 4. King, Joe, 19th cent.-Family. [G347].

JENNINGS -- Loeber, Charles. *Jennings Family, Garrard County, Kentucky. Address Delivered for the Jenning Family Record...at a Meeting Held in Garrod County Court House.* Lancaster, KY, Lancaster Central Record, 1929. 12p. [L9273].

JOHN -- John, D. D. *Historical Collections of the John Family in America.* Louisville, KY, 1951. 16p. Includes Binkley papers. [X-FW].

JOHN -- Jehn, Janet B. *Genealogy of Andrew Jehn and Barbara Gehred as of 1973.* Covington, KY, 1973. 38p. [X-FW].

JOINER -- Joiner, Ransey, Jr. *Joiner - Joyner: A History of Our Ancestors.* Mayfield, KY, 1973. 2 v. 347p. S does not show "2 v." [S1370; NG58].

JOLLY -- Baker, Nellie Fern. *Nelson Jolly Sr., and His Family of Breckenridge County,*

Kentucky. Baltimore, MD, Gateway Press, 1983. 241p. [C362; DS393].

JONES -- Hagan-Bowman, Mary E. *Ancestors-Descendants of John I. Jones Who Married Mary Ellen Swartzwelder (a McCann), Paris, Bourbon County, Ky.* NP. 1956. 19p. [X-DP/FW/MH/NY/OS/PH/SU/SW].

JONES -- Hannah, Esther Luce. *Kentucky Ancestors of My Mother, Maggie Jones.* Illinois, DAR, G.R.C. Genealogical Records Committee Report, Series 2, Vol. 8. NP, IL, 1988-89. [DC2024].

JONES -- Jones, Henry Earl. *The Jonses of Kentucky's Calloway & Marshall Counties, 1820-1910.* Fairhope, AL, Southern Mycology, Inc., 1988. 498p. 1. Jones family. 2. Calloway County (Ky.)-Genealogy. [G353; DC2026].

JONES -- Rollins, Kathleen. *A History and Genealogy of the Jones Family: from Kentucky and Across the United States.* Wickliffe, KY, K. Rollins, 1989. 78p. 1. Jones family. 2. Kentucky-Genealogy. [G354].

JORDAN -- Jordan, Warner R. *The Jordan, Caunter, Boyson, Jones Families as They Relate to Warner Jordan and Pearl Boyson Jordan.* Louisville, KY, Jordan, 1973. 39, 21 leaves. [D6950].

JOUETT -- Jonas, E. A. *Matthew Harris Jouett.* Louisville, KY, J. B. Speed Memorial Museum, 1938. viii, 118p. [D6953].

JOYNER -- Rogers, Erleen Joiner. *Seven Generations in and from Flatlick: The Thomas Joiner - Patience Webster Family Line through Israel G. Joiner.* Herndon, KY, E. J. Rogers, 1984. 120p. [C365].

JUSTICE -- Justice, Rara A. *Justine Genealogy; A Genalogical Record of the Justice Family Early Settlers of Pike County and Their Descendants.* Pikeville, KY, 1971. 399, 61p. [X-FW].

K

KARSNER -- Murphy, Margaret A. Karsner. *The Karsners of Kentucky.* Frankfort, KY, Tingle's Typesetting, 1981. xxx v. [D6978].

KAVANAUGH -- NAS. *Genealogical Table of the Kavanaugh Family; Early Marriages in Madison County, Ky., of the Kavanaugh Name Gleaned from the First Marriage Register of the County Court...* NP, n.d. 599-642p. Part 6 of History & Genealogies. [X-FW].

KEAHEY -- Reeves, Emma Barrett. *Keahey Clansmen Revisited.* Owensboro, KY, Cook & McDowell Publications, 1980. vi, 276p. Updated ed. of Keahey Clansmen and Their Kin, Slay, Summerall, Smith, 1969. [C370].

KEITH -- Claypool, E. A. *Records of Keith, Harned, and Irwin from Original Records (in Ky.)* Chicago, IL, 1902. 17p. [X-FW].

KEITH -- Young, Laurie. [G361]. See above: DONAHUE. [G195].

KELLEY -- Kelly, Mary Ann. *My Old Kentucky Home, Good-Night - 1st ed.* - Hicksville, NY, Exposition Press, 1979. xiii, 310p., 16 leaves of plates. 1. Kelley family. 2. Kelly, Mary Ann. 3. Ludlow (Ky.)-Biography. 4.Ludlow (Ky.)-History-Miscellanea. 5. Irish Americans-Kentucky-Ludlow-Biography. [G362].

KELLEY -- Pendergrass, Anita Ball. *That the Next Generation May Know: The Kelley's of Virginia and Kentucky.* Keokee, VA, 1973. 187p. NG lists as KELLY. [S1405; NG59; VV].

KENDALL -- Kendall, J. S. *Notes on the Kendall Family of Virginia, West Virginia, Kentucky, and Texas, with Reference to Allied Families.* Washington, DC, 1939. 1, 19, 21-98 numb. leaves. [L9585].

KENDALL -- Kendall, John S. *Notes on the Kendall Family of Virginia, West Virginia,*

Kentucky, and Texas, with Reference to Allied Families. New York, NY, 1939. 106 leaves. [X-NY; VV].

KENDALL -- Kendall, John Smith. *Kendall Family of Virginia, Kentucky, and Louisianna.* Berkeley, CA, 1945. 24 numb. l. [L9589].

KENDALL -- Kendall, John Smith. *The Kendall Family of Kentucky. Sketches Found in Historical Notes of Todd & Christian Counties.* Berkeley, CA, 1945. 12 l. [L9590].

KENDALL -- Kendall, John Smith. *A Collection of Notes, Letters and Genealogical Tables of the Kendall Family of Virginia, Maryland and Kentucky.* Berkeley, CA, 1945. 38 leaves. [L9591; VV].

KENDALL -- Miller, Caroline R. *The Kendalls and the Carringtons of Bath County, Kentucky.* Augusta, KY, C. R. Miller, 1984. 35, 20p. "A working paper designed to further research with these Bath County Families. [C375].

KERCHEVAL -- Parry, Guerdon G. *Something About the Kercheval Family.* Frankfort, KY, 1924. (195) - 202p. Reprinted from the "Register of the Kentucky State Historical Soc." May, 1924. [X-PH].

KERN -- Garrard, Mary Margaret Kern. *The Kern Family of Rowan County, North Carolina; Nicholas County, Kentucky; Boone, Clinton,, Lawrence, Monroe Counties, Indiana; Hancock County, Illinois, Lee County, Iowa.* Noblesville, IN, 1968. 53p. [L9643; D7094].

KESSLER -- Wright, Eunice Montgomery. *Isabella Berry, 1845-1889, and Husband, Daniel M. Kessler and Their Descendnats.* Campbellsville, KY, E. M. Wright, 1985. 29 leaves. 1. Kessler family. 2. Kessler, Isabella Berry, 1845-1889-Family. [G366].

KETCHAM -- Armbrust, Janet Lee Ketchum. *A Gathering of Ketchum Kindred: The Descendants* *of Benjamin and Rhoda (Benn) Ketchum of Decatur County, Indiana: Including Other Ketchum/Ketcham Families of Ohio, Indiana, and Kentucky.* Mount Vernon, WA, J.L.K. Armbrust, 1990. viii, 167p. 1. Ketcham family. 2. Ketchum, Benjamin, 1840-1888-Family. 3. Ketchum, Rhoda, 1807-1888-Family. 4. Middle West-Genealogy. [G367].

KIDWELL -- Kidwell, Harold. *Kidwell Families of Kentucky - 1st ed. -* Twentynine Palms, CA, Desert Moon Press, 1990. 186p. 1. Kidwell family. 2. Kentucky-Genealogy. [G367].

KILGORE -- Carpenter, Evelyn Yates. *Thomas Kilgore, Sr., and His Proven Descendants to 1991.* Bowling Green, KY, Yates, 1991. 279p. [DC2097].

KINCAID -- Hines, Sallye Lathram. *Deep Roots. History and Genealogy of the Kincaid - Coyle - Darnell - Lathram -Hart Families and Related Families, 1064-1964.* Lexington, KY, The Letter Shop, 1964. 159p. [D7171; X-FW].

KING -- Jenkins, Rella Gibbs. [G370]. See above: JENKINS. [G347].

KITTERMAN -- Perry, Virginia Shoemaker. *Kitterman Sinew: The Genealogy and Story of the Life of Christopher Kitterman, His Family, and Their Descendants.* Utica, KY, McDowell Publications, 1986. 972p. 1. Kitterman family. 2. Kitterman, Christopher, ca. 1732-1805 or 6-Family. [G372].

KLEIN -- Brzoska, Ellen. *The Cline Book: Being Descendants of Levi Cline and Elizabeth McClaskey of Carroll County, Indiana, with Some Records of John Cline of Shelby County, Kentucky and His Children.* Yakima, WA, Priv. Print. by Stanley and Ellen Brzoska and Karen Hiatt, 1982. viii, 881p. [C384].

KLEIN -- Crabb, Opal Cline. *George Cline Family History.* Utica, KY, McDowell Publications, 1984. x, 163p. 1. Klein family. 2. Cline, George Washington, 1847-1918-Family. [G372].

KUYKENDALL -- Kuykendall, Jerry M. *Andrew Kuykendall from Kentucky: A Family History.* Filer, ID, Kuykendall, 1977. xiii, 252p., 35 leaves of plates. [C393].

L

LAING -- Ward, Azuba Ruth. *The Laing Family.* Lexington, KY, Ward, 1991. x, 333p. [DC2156].

LAIR -- Lafferty, Maude Ward & Helen Lafferty Nisbet. *Background of the Lair Family, 1738-1958.* Lexington, KY, The Authors, 1958, 1966. 62p. L shows 1958. [L9982; NG61: DC2157].

LANCASTER -- Lancaster, Jeannie. *Lancaster Family of Trigg County, Kentucky: Descendants of Levi & Faith (Futrell) Lancaster.* Hopkinsville, KY, J. Lancaster, 1988. 282, 63p., 1 leaf of plates. 1. Lancster family. 2. Lancaster, Levi, 1774-1844-Family. 3. Kentucky-Genealogy. [G385].

LANCASTER -- Lancaster, Samuel V. *The Lancaster Family of Maryland and Kentucky. A History of the English Ancestry Emigrating to the Colony of Maryland.* NP, Lancaster, 1970. 200p. [D7402; X-FW].

LANDER -- Lander, David. *History of the Lander Family of Virginia and Kentucky.* Chicago, IL, Regan Printing House, 1926. 213p. [D7405; X-FW; VV].

LANE -- Dearinger, David B. *The Descendants of Edward and Rhoda Lane of Anderson County, Kentucky.* NP, 1984. 271 l. [DC2168].

LANGFORD -- Maes, Virginia Ingles. *The Descendants of John Frederick Langford of Great Britain, Indiana, and Illinois and His Wife Mary Adams of Kentucky and Illinois to* *the Sixth Generation.* Rushville, IN, 1942. 14 leaves. [L10068].

LANHAM -- Lanham, Hugh Asa. *The Lanham History.* Harrodsubrg, KY, Britton's Printing Service, 1972. iii, 200p. [D7438].

LANTER -- Robinson, Mary Lois. *The Genealogy of the Lanter Family, 1700-1983. 1st ed.* Danville, KY, M. L. Robinson. 1938. 298, 28p., 32 pages of plates. [C400].

La RUE -- Mather, Otis M. *Six Generations of La Rues and Allied Families: Containing Sketch of Isaac La Rue, Senior, Who Died in Frederick County, Virginia, in 1795,and Some Account of His American Ancestors and Three Generations of His Descendants and Families Who were Connected by Intermarriage, among others, Carman, Hodgen, Helm, Buzan, McDonald, Castleman, Walters, Alexander, Medley, McMahon, Vertrees, Keith, Wintersmith, Clay, Neill, Grantham, Vanmeter, and Enlow; Copies of Six Old Wills and Other Documents; Various Incedents Connected with the Settlement of Nolynn Valley in Kentucky; also a Chapter on the La Rue Family and the Child of Abraham Lincoln.* Hodgenville, KY, Mather (Louisville, KY, C. T. Dearing Printing.), 1921. xiii, 198p. [L10102; D7463; VV].

LASHBROOK -- Lashbrook, Mary K. Gritt. *Lashbrooke, Lashbrooks, and Lashbrook (of the United States).* Utica, KY, McDowell Publications, 1986. vii, 326p. [G389].

LASLIE -- Tibiletti, Mary Laslie. *From the Hills of Kentucky.* Beaver Dam, KY, Embrys Newspapers, 1965. 186p. [X-DP].

LAWRENCE -- Lawrence, James Reed. *A Kentucky Pioneer Family: The Lawrences and Their Kin.* Deatsville, KY, Lawrence, 1984. 291p. [DC2186].

LAWSON -- Clark, Lillian Bond. *The Lawson Family of Scioto County, Ohio and Greenup*

County, Kentucky. Portsmouth, OH, Clark, 1976. 64p. [D7500].

LAWSON -- Doss, Brenda Collier. *The Lawson Family.* Powderly, KY, B. C. Doss, 1984. 79, 5p. [C404].

LEDFORD -- Egerton, John. *Generations: An American Family.* Lexington, KY, University of Kentucky, 1983. 263p. [C406; DC2208].

LEE -- Fontaine, Wm. Winston. *The Descendants of General Robert E. Lee, From King Robert the Bruce, of Scotland.* A paper read before the Southern Historical Association, of Louisville, KY., March 29, 1881. NP, 1881. 6p., 1 leaf. "Descendants of Governor Spotswood and his wife"; 1 leaf at end. [L10246; VV].

LEESE -- Leese, Charles. *The Lawrence Leese Family History; Two Centuries in America (1741-1941); A Biographical and Genealogical History of Lawrence Leese and His Descendants From the Time of His Arrival in the City of Philadelphia Through a Period of Two Hundred Years Down to the Ninth Generation.* Frankfort, KY, Roberts Printing Co., 1941. 214p. [L10303; D7580].

LEONARD -- Bailey, Jack Dalton. [G397]. See above: DEVINE. [G187].

LEONARD -- Townsend, John W. *Life of James Francis Leonard, the First Practical Sound-Reader of the Morse Alphabet...* Louisville, KY, J. P. Morton, 1909, 85p. Filson Club Publications, No. 24 Pt. 1. [X-FW].

LETTON -- Watson, Estelle Osborn (Clark). *Some Lettons and Willetts of Maryland; and Allied Families: Layton, Leighton, Letten, Leyton, Liten, Litten, Litton, Lytton.* Louisville, KY, 1955. 43p. [L10430; NG62].

LEWIS -- NAS. *Lewis Congress, 1894. Celebration of the Two Hundredth Anniversary of Their Residence in Virginia by the Lewis*

Family at Bel Air, Spotsylvania County, September 4, 1894. Frankfort, KY, G. A. Lewis Printer, 1894. variously paged. [A395].

LEWIS -- Hodges, Glen. *Daybreak on Old Fortification Creek: A History of John Lewis, His Family and Descendants.* Hawesville, KY, Hancock County Historical Society, 1989. 157p. 1. Lewis family. 2. Hancock County (Ky.)-Biography. 3. Hancock County (Ky.)-Genealogy. 4. Hancock County (Ky.)-History. [G399; DC2237].

LEWIS -- Lewis, George A. *Celebration of the Two Hundreth Anniversary of Their Residence in Virginia by the Lewis Family in Bel-Air, Spotsylvania Country, September 4th, 1894.* Frankfort, KY, Geo. A. Lewis, 1894. 1 v. in various pagings. [DS431].

LEWIS -- Lewis, William Terrell. *Genealogy of the Lewis Family in America from the Middle of the Seventeenth Century to the Present Time.* Louisville, KY, Pub. by Courier Journal Job Printing Co., 1893. 454p. [A394].

LEWIS -- Merrill, Boynton. *Jefferson's Nephews: A Frontier Tragedy.* Princeton, NJ, Princeton University Press, 1976. xv, 462p. 1. Livingston County (Ky.)-History. 2. Lewis, Isham, d. 1815. 3. Lewis, Lilburn, d. 1812. 4. Lewis family. 5. Murder-Kentucky-Livingston County-Case Studies. [G399].

LEWIS -- Merrill, Boynton. *Jefferson's Nephews: A Frontier Tragedy - 2nd ed. with a New Preface.* Lexington, KY, University Press of Kentucky, 1987. xvi, 462p. 1. Livingston County (Ky.)-History. 2. Lewis, Isham, d. 1815. 3. Lewis, Lilburn, d. 1812. 4. Lewis family. 5. Murder-Kentucky-Livingston County-Case Studies. [G399].

LEWIS -- Purcell, Martha Grossham. *Lucy Jefferson Lewis, Sister of President Thomas Jefferson; Virginia 1752 - Kentucky, 1811.* NP, 1924. 16p, 1 leaf. [L10458].

LEWIS -- Van Meter, Benjamin F. *Genealogies and Sketches of Some Old Families Who Have Taken Prominent Part in the Development of Virginia and Kentucky Especially, and Later of Many Other States in this Union.* Louisville, KY, J. P. Morton & Co., 1901. 183p. [A397; VV].

LIGON -- Miller, Margaret Hardwick. *Ligons and Their Kin of Graves County, Ky.* Corsicana, TX, Miller, 197_. 133 leaves. [D7691].

LIGON -- Pearce, Marvin J., Sr. *Ligon Pioneers in Kentucky.* El Cerrito, CA, Pearce, 1967. 104p. [NG63; D7692].

LILE -- Martin, John R. *Lile - Turner. Descendants of John Martin Lile (1795-1870) of Clark County, Ky. and Macon County, MO.* Morton, IL, 1970. 204p, 18 leaves. [X-DP/FW].

LINCOLN -- NAS. *Sarah Bush Lincoln, the Beloved Foster Mother of Abraham Lincoln; A Memorial.* Elizabethtown, KY, Elizabethtown Woman's Club. 1922. 8p. [L10514].

LINCOLN -- NAS. *Lincoln Kinsman. July, 1938 - Dec. 1942.* Fort Wayne, IN, Lincolnians Pub., No. 1-54 in vol. 1. [X-FW].

LINCOLN -- Barton, Rev. William E. *The Man Who Married Lincoln's Parents... Delivered at the Dedication of a Monument at the Grave of Rev. Jesse Head and Jane Ramsey Head, His Wife, in Spring Hill Cemetary, Harrodsburg, Kentucky, Thursday, November 2, 1922.* Harrodsburg, KY, The Harrodsburg Herald, 1922. 16p. [L10512].

LINCOLN -- Barton, William E. *The Parents of Abraham Lincoln,... Delivered at the Grave of Thomas Lincoln, Goose Nest Prairie,... Illinois, September 18, 1922.* Charlestton, IL., The Charleston Daily Courier, 1922. 8p. [L10513].

LINCOLN -- Barton, William E. *The Lincolns in Their Old Kentucky Home; An Address Delivered Before the Filson Club, Louisville, Kentucky, December 4, 1922.* Berea, KY, Berea College Press, 1923. 24p. [L10515: L10530].

LINCOLN -- Barton, William E. *'Old Theories Upset', Being a Brief Report on an Address on Abraham Lincoln's Lost Grandmother...Before... the Chicago Historical Society.* Chicago, IL, 1923. 30, 4p. [L10516].

LINCOLN -- Barton, William Eleazer. *The Lincoln Family in America. (In the Magazine of History).* Tarrytown, NY, 1925. No. 113 (v.29 no.1). [L10519].

LINCOLN -- Barton, William E. *The Lineage of Lincoln...* Indianapolis, IN, The Bobbs-Merrill Company, 1929. 14, 419p. [L10520].

LINCOLN -- Brinkley, Phyllis C. *The Lincolns: Targets of Controversy. 1st ed.* Waunakee, WI, P. Brinkley, 1985. 77p. [C415].

LINCOLN -- Egle, William H. *Pennsylvania Ancestry of President Lincoln. (Manuscript Copy from the Original Possession of Robert T. Lincoln, of Chicago, copied by Harriet Henton, 1902.).* NP, n.d. 44, 2 leaves. [X-FW].

LINCOLN -- Fearing, Charles W. *Contemporary Kindred of Abraham Lincoln; A Paper read at...the Weymouth Historical Society, March 29, 1928.* Weymouth, MA, 1929. 53p, 3 l. [L10522].

LINCOLN -- Gwynnee, Jacob M. *The Cousin Connection and Genealogy of Abraham Lincoln, 16th President of the United States and Abraham Lincoln of Fayette County, Pennsylvania.* Willingboro, NJ, Gwynne, 1976. iii. 30p. [X-PH].

LINCOLN -- Horton, Howard Leavitt. *Abraham Lincoln.* Boston, 1950. 25 l. [L10541].

LINCOLN -- Lea, J. Henry and J. R. Hutchinson. *The Ancestry of Abraham Lincoln.*Boston and New York, Houghton, Mifflin Company, 1909. xvi, 212p. [L10508].

LINCOLN -- Lewis, Montgomery S. *Legends That Libel Lincoln.* New York, Toronto, Rinehart & Company, Inc., 1946. xiii, 239p. [L10538].

LINCOLN -- Lyda, Forrest Edgar. *Abraham Lincoln: A Local Tradition.* __, KY, Lyda, 1977. 7p. (HendersonCounty Genealogical Workbook, ser., 1; no. 3. [C415].

LINCOLN -- Mather, Otis May. *The Mather Papers; Pertaining Mainly to the History of Hodgenville, Ky., History of LaRue County's Most Illustrious Son.* Hodgenville, Ky., LaRue Co. Herald-News, 1968. 45p. 1. Hodgenville (Ky.) 2. LaRue County (Ky.) 3. Lincoln family. [G401].

LINCOLN -- McMurtry, R. Gerald. *The Lincolns in Elizabethtown, Kentucky.* Fort Wayne, IN, Lincolniana Publishers, 1932. 16p. [L10528].

LINCOLN -- McMurtry, R. Gerald. *A Series of Monographs Concerning the Lincolns and Hardin County, Kentucky.* Elizabethtown, KY, Enterprise Press, 1938. 4. 133p. [L10533; D7707].

LINCOLN -- McMurtry, Robert G. *Kentucky Lincolns on Mill Creek.* Harrogate, TN, Lincoln Memorial Univ., 1939. 78p. [X-FW].

LINCOLN -- Peterson, James Andrew. *Abraham Lincoln: Some Kentucky Background.* Yorkville, IL, Peterson, 1976. 79p. 200 copies printed. [C415; DC2261].

LINCOLN -- Sandel, Elias Wesley. *Lincoln, Man of Destiny.* Florien, LA, E. W. Sandel, 1989. 186p. "With genealogical charts on Lincolns, Todd, and related families of

Sparrow, Shipley, Bates, Hanks, Gurley (his pastor), Rutledge, Herndon (friend), Isham,Johnston, Hall, Beckwith. 1. Lincoln, Abraham, 1809-1965. 2. Presidents-United States-Biography. 3. Lincoln, Abraham, 1809-1865-Family. 4. Lincoln family. 5. Todd family. [G401].

LINCOLN -- Semones, Hattie. *Duel with Destiny.* Radford, VA, Commonwealth Press, 1976. viii, 131p. [C415].

LINCOLN -- Shackford, Samuel. *The Lineage of President Lincoln.* Boston, 1887. 7p. [L10502].

LINCOLN -- Simon, John Y. *House Divided: Lincoln and His Father.* Fort Wayne, IN, Louis A. Warren Lincoln Library and Museum, 1987. 30p. (The Tenth annual R. Gerald McMurtry lecture). 1. Lincoln, Abraham, 1809-1865-Family. 2. Lincoln, Thomas, 1778-1851. 3. Lincoln family. 4. Presidents-United States-Biography. 5. Presidents-United States-Fathers-Biography. [G402].

LINCOLN -- Suppiger, Joseph E. *The Intimate Lincoln.* Lanham, MD, University Press of America, 1985. vii, 259p. [C415].

LINCOLN -- Tarbell, Ida M. *In the Footsteps of the Lincolns.* New York and London, Harper & Brothers, 1924. xi, 2, 418p. [L10518].

LINCOLN -- Tyler, Lyon Gardiner. *Barton and the Lineage of Lincoln, Claim that Lincoln Was Related to Lee Refuted...2nd ed.* NP, 1930. 12p. [L10525].

LINCOLN -- Warren, Louis A. *Hananiah Lincoln in Revolution and Pioneer History.* Bloomington, IN, University Press, 1929. Various pagings. [L10521].

LINCOLN -- Warren, Louis A. *The Lincoln and LaFollette Families in Pioneer Drama.* Menasha, WI, 1929. 23p. [L10523].

LINCOLN -- Warren, Louis A. *Pilgrimage Conducted June 20 - 30, 1937...on the 300th Anniversary of the Lincolns Landing in America; Including the Meeting at Long Run Baptist Church, Jefferson County, Near the Site of the Home of Pioneer Abraham Lincoln; Sponsored by the Filson Club, Louisville, Kentucky, Inc. June, 25, 1937.* Louisville, KY, J. P. Morton & Co., 1937. 16p. Includes: The Lincolns in Jefferson County, Kentucky by R.C.B. Thruston. [L10531].

LINCOLN -- Warren, Louis A. *Three Generations of Kentucky Lincolns.* Fort Wayne, IN, Lincolniana Publishers, 1938. (65) - 78p. Reprint from the Filson Club Quarterly, v. 12, no. 2. [X-FW/MH].

LINDSAY -- Lindsey, Helen Bradley. *Early Settlers in Campbell County, Ky. Lindsey, McPike, Noble.* Newport, KY, 1927. 22p. [L10559].

LINDSAY -- Sparacio, Ruth Trickey and Sam. *Pamunkey Neighbors of Orange Country, Virginia: Transcription From the Original Files of County Courts in Virginia, Kentucky, and Missouri of Wills, Deeds, Order Books & Marriages as well as Some Family Lines; Lindsay, Mills, Mountague, Stevens, and Related Families and Neighbors.* Baltimore, Gateway Press, 1985. xiv, 597p. 1. Lindsay family. 2. Mills family. 3. Montague family. 4. Orange County (Va.)-Genealogy. 5. Court records-Virginia-Orange County. [G403: C416; VV].

LINDSAY -- Wood, Forest Patrick. *The Lindsay - Lindsey Family of Pa., Va., Ky, and Ind.* Seattle, WA, Wood, 1966. 20 leaves. [D7721; VP; VV].

LINDSEY -- Lindsey, Helen B. *Thomas Noble Lindsey and Descendants.* Newport, KY, or Cincinnati, OH, 1928. 8p. [X-FW/MH].

LINN -- Wade, Daraleen Phillips. *Linn - McDannald Being Some of the Ancestors and*

Descendants of Philip E. and Mahala (McDannald) Linn, Principally in Kentucky, Illinois, and Oregon. NP, 1984. 173p. [NG63].

LINNEY -- Linney, James Erle. *Genealogy of the Linney Family in England, Virginia, Maryland... and Possibly Other States.* Harrodsburg, KY, Harrodsburg Herald, 1974. xviii, 237p. [S1590; VV].

LINVILLE -- Moore, Thelbert R. *I Am Related to the Linnvilles; A Linville Genealogy.* Mt. Olivet, KY, Author, n.d. 103p. 42 leaves. [X-FW].

LIST -- Tingle, Mary Alice. *List Genealogy.* __, KY, M. A. Tingle, 1979. ca. 150 leaves. [C418].

LITTLE -- Little, Julius. *Isaac Little and His Descendants.* McMurray, PA, J. Little, 1985. viii, 24 l. 1. Little family. 2. Little, Isaac, ca. 1760-ca. 1823-Family. 3. Kentucky-Genealogy. 4. Pennsylvania-Genealogy. [G404].

LIVELY -- Louden, Claire Humphfres. *Second Supplement to Livelys of America, 1690-1868, and to Supplement to Lively of America 1972.* McMinnville, TN, National Association of Lively Families, Ashland, KY, Gallahers, 1986. 1071-1998p. 1. Lively family. I. Marsh, Alta Lively, 1926- II. Livelys of America 1982. III. Livelys of America, 1690-1968. IV. Supplement to Livelys of America 1972. [G405].

LOGAN -- Barry, Byrdella Logan. *Timothy Logan of North Carolina and Kentucky.* NP, 1953. 37 l. [D7806].

LOGAN -- Green, Thomas Marshall. *The Logans. (In Historic Families of Kentucky...1st Series).* Cincinnati, OH, 1889. p117-229. [L10659].

LONG -- Long, James L. *Short History of the Long Family.* Shelbyville, KY, Shelby Sentinel, 1898. 134p. [X-FW].

LOPP -- Beanblossom, Walter S. *The Lopps of Harrison County, Indiana.* Hawesville, KY, Beanblossom, Beanblossom, 1972. iii leaves, 411p. [D7844].

LOTT -- Young, Laurie. [G409]. See above: DONAHUE. [G195].

LOWE -- Costigan, Patrick W. *William Lowe of Drake's Creek, Simpson County, Kentucky.* Minneapolis, MN, 1982. 9 leaves. [NG64].

LOWE -- McDuffie, Eva Loe. *The Lowe - Loe - Low Family in Virginia, North Carolina, Mississippi, Tennessee, Kentucky, and Missouri.* NP, 1955. 109 leaves. [D7888; VV].

LUNSFORD -- Lunsford, Ralph W., Mrs. *The Lunsford Family of England and America.* Utica, KY, McDowell Publications, 1982. 60p. [G412].

LUSBY -- Koch, Edna L. *Lusby - Risk Families: Some Descendants of William Lusby (ca1755-1815) and William Risk (1774-1854) both of Clark County, Kentucky.* Portland, OR, Genealogical Forum of Portland, Oregon, 1982. xiv, 186p. [C427].

LUSK -- Dixon, Dexter. *Lusks, A Pioneer Family.* Blackey, KY, D. Dixon, 198_. 96 l. 1. Lusk family. 2. Kentucky-Genealogy. [G413].

LUTTRELL -- Martin, Mrs Guy. *Descendants of Thomas Luttrell with Tabitha Rutherford of Kentucky and Illinois.* Waverly, IL, Martin,Woods, 1967. 1 v. (various pagings). [D7941].

LYONS -- Doss, Brenda Collier. *The Lyons Family.* Utica, KY, McDowell Publications, 1985. iv, 187, 15p. [C429].

LYONS -- Doss, Brenda Collier. *Abraham J., Jr. & Elizabeth Matilda (Sharp) Lyons and Their Descendants. Limited ed.* Utica, KY,

McDowell Publications, 1985. 340, 14p., 1 leaf of plates. 1. Lyons family. 2. Lyons, Abraham J., 1822-1868-Family. 3. Kentucky-Genealogy. [G414].

M

MACBRYDE -- Dixon, Ben F. ...*A McBride Chronology, With a Perspective View of the Findings, a Series of Notices on "McBride" From the Public Records of Early Virginia and Kentucky, Chronologically Arranged with an Interpretation of Their Evidence.* Washington, DC, 1941. [VV].

MACDONALD -- Williams, Mrs. Flora McDonald. *The Glengarry McDonalds of Virginia with an Introductory Sketch of the Early History of the Glengarry Clan.* Louisville, KY, G. G. Fetter Company, 1911. [L11033].

MACE -- DeMarce, Virginia Easley. *Clues to the Ancestry of Solomon Mace of Boone Co., Mo., the Mase / Mace Family of Ralls and Pike Cos., Mo., the Mase / Mace Family of Bourbon and Bath Cos., Ky., the Mace Family of Hampshire/Hardy Cos., Va./W.Va. Preliminary Draft.* Arlington, VA, J. L. DeMarce, 1989. 41 leaves. 1 Mace family. 2. Mace, Solomon, 1819-1854-Family. 3. Missouri Genealogy. 4. Kentucky-Genealogy. 5. West Virginia-Genealogy. [G415].

MACGREGOR -- Locker, Ora B. *McGregor Genealogy.* Paducah, KY, 1962. 128p. [X-FW/NY].

MACKEYS -- Hoskinson, Josie V. H. & Bishop, Julia R. *Mackeys and Eberleys of Texas and Allied Families of McIlwaine, Elgin, Harrison, Adams, Smallwood, Stone, Troope, and Perry of KY., TENN., MD., and VA.* Norman, OK, 1965. xii, 172p. X libraries list under MACKEY. [NG67; X-FW/GF/NY].

MAHURIN -- NAS. *The Mahurin Family, A Family History and Genealogical Record of*

Stephen Mahurin (1774-1849) of Grayson County, Kentucky: His Descendants to Date and His Ancestors to Hugh Mahurin (1690-1718) of Tauunton (sic) Massachusetts. Bethesda, MD, 1959. 91p. [L11340].

MAJOR -- Downing, George C. *The Major Genealogy of Franklin County, Ky. Descendants of John Major.* Roanoke, VA, Record Print, 1958. 10p. LA give no date. [X-LA; VV].

MANION -- Dinn, Ruth. *Descendants of Edmond Manion, VA, KY, IN.* Franklin, IN, Dinn, 1974. 158p. [DC2352; X-FW].

MARSHALL -- Marshall, Janet H. *Marshall Family History.* Lexington, KY, J. D. Marshall, 1985. 130p., 1 leaf. of plates. [G425].

MARTIN -- Brinkley, Beatrice Martin. *Records of Martin - Crawford - Rodes - Dishman Families in Virginia, Kentucky and Texas.* NP, 1972. 193 leaves. [D8147; VV].

MARTIN -- Martin, Claude O. *Martin Records of the Families of Peter Martin of Prussia, Va. & Ky.; Sarah Redding Martin of Eng., Va., Ky, and John Martin of Va. & Ky. & Sarah Jefferson Martin of Va., Ky., and Ind.* Madera, CA, 196_. 82p. [X-FW; VV].

MARTIN -- Martin, Samuel D. *Genealogical Record of the Martin Family.* Pine Grove, KY, 1857. 8p. [L11471].

MARTIN -- Martin, Walter S. *Martin Family Record, from 1760-1963.* Garrett, KY, H. Conley; Richmond, KY, H. G. Martin, 1979. 1983 printing. 311p. 1. Martin family. 2. Kentucy-Genealogy. [G426; C441].

MARTIN -- Souder, Marjorie Ann Martin. *Peter Martin, 1741-1807: A Revolutionary War Soldier of Virginia Buried in Shelby County, Kentucky: His Washington County, Indiana, and Many Other Descendants.* Pekin, IN, M. A. M.

Souder, 445p. 1. Martin family. 2. Martin, Peter, 1741-1807-Family. [G427].

MARTIN -- Watson, Estelle Clark. *Some Martin, Jeffries, and Wayman Families and Connections of Virginia, Maryland, Kentucky, and Indiana.* Skokie, IL, Guild Press, Inc., 1965. 273p. [D8169; VV].

MASON -- NAS. *The William Mason Family of Casey County, Kentucky, Edgar Country Illinois, Knox County, Missouri.* NP, 1968. 10 leaves. [L11541].

MASSEY -- Smith, Carmae Massey. *Descendants of Arthur Massey, Cheraws District, South Carolina, 1769.* Owensboro, KY, Cook-McDowell Publications, Inc., 1980. 193p. [C444; D8200].

MASSIE -- Kelsey, Mavis Parrott and Mary Wilson Kelsey. *The Family of John Massie, 1743-c1830, Revolutionary Patriot of Louisa Country, Virginia. Early Emigrants to KY and TX, Bachman, Baker, Bollinger, Burris Clopton, Duke, Harris, Jackson, Keener, Overton, Parrott, Poer, Riddel, and Walton Families.* Houston, TX, Kelsey, 1979. 241p. C lists under MASSEY. [C443; NG69; D8201].

MASSIE -- Martin, Myra Nichols. *History of William, Jeremiah & Alfred Massie of Kentucky & Illinois.* NP, 1967. 50 l. [D8202].

MATHIS -- Edwards, Richard Laurence. [G429]. See above: EDWARDS. [G208].

MATTHEWS -- Matthews, Mitchell Dudley. *The Matthews and Mitchell Families of May's Lick Ky., and Power and Dudley Families of Flemingsburg, Ky.* Pearl Harbor, T. H., 1940. 1 v. [L11586].

MATTHEWS -- Matthews, Mitchell Dudley. *Walter Matthews of May's Lick, Kenctucky.* Princeton, NJ, Four Bears Press, 1968. 66p. [D8237].

MAXEY -- White, Emery H. *The Barrens: A Family History of South Central Kentucky.* Glasgow, KY, E. H. White, 1986. 111p. 1. White family. 2. Maxey family. 3. Pope family. [G431].

MAY -- May, B. David. *Our Family Heritage: Some East Kentucky Roots.* Baltimore, MD, Gateway Press, v. <1 >. Contents v. 1. The Descendants of Caleb and Margaretta (Patrick) May, 1781-1985. 1. May family. 2. Kentucky-Genealogy. [G431].

MAY -- May, B. David. *The Descendants of Caleb and Margaretta (Patrick) May, 1781-1985.* Baltimore, MD, Gateway Press, v. 470p., 3 leaves of plates. 1. May family. 2. May, Caleb, 1780 or 81-1827-Family. 3. Kentucky-Genealogy. [G431].

MAY -- Woodruff, Audrey L. W. *Descendants of John May, Sr. and Sarah Jane (Phillips) May, 1760-1967 of Virginia, Tenn., Kentucky... and Allied Families of Hanson, Wall, Rook, Mundell.* Kansas City, MO?, 1967. 62p. [X-FW; VV].

MAYER -- Seaman, Sallyann Jean. *John Nicholas Mayer and All Known Descendants.* Owensboro, KY, McDowell Publications, 1981. 140p. [DS464].

MAYHEW -- Mayhew, Eva Mae. *Bridges to the Mayhew Past.* Allen Co., KY, E. M. Mayhew, 1985. 387p., 23p.of plates. 1. Mayhew family. 2. Vincent, Patricia Mayhew, 1951- [G432].

MAYNARD -- Maynard, Roland B. *The Maynards of East Kentucky from Pioneers to the Tenth Generation. -- 1st ed.* Pikeville, KY, Pike County Historical Society, 1979. xi, 354p., 4 pages of plates. [C448; DC2414].

McADOO -- Lemons, Nova A. *John McAdoo of Virginia, North Carolina, Tennessee, and Kentucky.* Dallas, TX, Lemons, 1991. iv, 52p. [DC2424].

McADAMS -- McAdams, Pope. *Some Ancestors of Eugene Perrot McAdams and Mary Elizabeth Pope McAdams of Hawesville, Kentucky. Also Cocke and Pope Families.* Shively, KY, 1936. 433p. [L10904; NG65].

McBRIDE -- Dixon, Benjamin F. *McBride Family of Virginia and Kentucky, and the Rout Family of Kentucky.*Washington, DC, 1971. 2 leaves, 11p. [X-FW; VV].

McCANN -- NAS. *Some Descendnts of John Keaund of Whithorn Scotland, Many of Whom Lived and Died in Paris, Bourbon County, Ky. and Were Known as McCanns. (With Collateral Lineages of McNitt, (McNaughtons), Penn, Sunderland, and Wrights.* Hopewell, VA, 1953. Various Pagings. [X-NY/OS].

McCANN -- McCann, Robert Lee and William Ray McCann. *Family of Eliza R. McCann, Who Married Lytle Griffing; Bourbon County, Kentucky, Adams County, Illinois. With Index.* Hopewell, VA, 1963. 75p. [L10938].

McCANN -- McCann, W. R. *Some Descendants of John Keand of Whithorn, Scotland, Many of Whom Lived and Died in Paris, Bourbon County, Kentucky, and Were Known as McCanns.* NP, 1953. 30, 25 leaves. [D8333].

McCANN -- McCann, William R. *Family of Wesley D. McCann, Bourbon County, Ky, and Adams Co., Ill.* NP, 1962. 12p. [X-FW].

McCANN -- McCann, William Ray. *Some Descendants of John Keand of Whithorn,, Scotland and Paris, Bourbon County, Kentucky. McCann family.* NP, 1955. 1 v. [NG65].

McCHESNEY -- Schultz, Katherine E. *The McChesneys of Caldwell County, Kentucky.* Annville, PA, 1969. 82 leaves. [A421].

McCHORD -- McChord, J. H. *The McChords of Kentucky and Some Related Families: The Hynes, Caldwell, Wickliffe, Hardin, McElroy,*

Shuck, and Irvine Families. Louisville, KY, Westerfield Bonte Co., 1941. ii, 56p. [L10951].

McCLANAHAN -- Pompey, Sherman Lee. *The Genealogy of Eli Clark McClanahan of Bracken County, Kentucky.* Florence, OR, Western Oregon Genealogica Research Library, 1981. 3 leaves. [C450].

McCLOSKEY -- McClaskey, Michael J. *Descendants of James McClaskey of Nelson County, Kentucky.* Idaho Falls, ID, M. J. McClaskey, 1981. 104 leaves. [C451].

McCLOSKEY -- McClaskey, Kenneth L., Barbara M., and Michael J. *McClaskeys in Military History.* Idaho Falls, ID, M. J. McClaskey and B. M. McClaskey, 1981. v. <2 >. [C451].

McCLURE -- Lloyd, Emma Rouse. *McClure (McLure) Family of Kentucky.* (Available for Consultation at the Lloyd Library, 309 West Court St., Cincinnati, OH. NP, n.d., pagination not shown. [L10969].

McCLURE -- McClure, Stanley W. *The McClure Family: A Record of McClure Families of Harrison County, Kentucky, Frankline County, Indiana, Hamilton County, Ohio, Junction City, Kansas and Other Lines of Descent.* NP, 1956. 26 leaves. [G435].

McCLURE -- McClure, Stanley W. *The McClure Family: A Record of McClure Families of Harrison County, Kentucky, Frankline County, Indiana, Hamilton County, Ohio, Junction City, Kansas and Other Lines of Descent -- Rev. --.* Harrison, OH, S. W. McClure, 1983. 52 l. [C451].

McCLURE -- Venard, Daniel Lloyd. *Kentucky McClures in McDonough County, Illinois.* Macomb, IL, D. L. Venard, 1985. 23 leaves. 1. McClure family. 2. McDonough County (Ill.)-Family. 3. Kentucky-Genealogy. [G435].

McCORMICK -- McCormick, Andrew Phillip. *Scotch-Irish in Ireland and America, as Shown in Sketches of the Pioneer Scotch-Irish Families McCormick, Stevenson, McKenzie, and Bell in North Carolina, Kentucky, Missouri and Texas.* New Orleans, LA, 1897. 2. 174, 72p., 1 leaf. [L10983].

McCOY -- McCoy, Lycurgus. *William McCoy and His Descendants; A Genealogical History of the Family of William McCoy, One of the Scotch Families Coming to America Before the Revolutionary War, Who Died in Kentucky about the Year 1818. Also a History of the Family of Alexander McCoy, A Scotsman Who Served through the Revolutionary War, and Died in Ohio in the Year 1820.* Battle Creek, MI, McCoy, 1904. 204p. [L10992].

McCOY -- McCoy, Truda Williams. *The McCoys: Their Story As Told to the Author by Eyewitnesses and Descendants; Edited and with a Foreword by Leonard Roberts -- 1st ed. --* Pikeville, KY, Preservation Council Press of the Preservation Council of Pike County, 1976. xii, 338p, 16 leaves. of plates. Errata sheet inserted. [G436; C453; X-FW/NY].

McCOY -- McCoy, Hobart and Orville. *Squirrel Huntin' Sam: His Memoir and a Family Tree. -- 1st ed. --* Pikeville, KY, Pikeville College Press, 1979. 181p. Errata slip inserted. 1. McCoy Sam. 2. Hatfield - McCoy feud. 3. McCoy family. 4. Pike County (Ky.)-Biography. [G436; C453].

McCUDDY -- Peters, Norman R. *The McCuddy Family of Maryland and Kentucky.* Washington, DC, 1988. 20p. [NGS8].

McCUNE -- Knapp, Alfred Averill & Mrs Amy Edna (Ramey) McCune (Mrs. Lewis). *Some of the Descendants of Robert and Jane McCune of Bourbon and Nicholas Counties, Kentucky.* Winter Park, FL, College Press, 1947. 57p. [L11007].

McCUNE -- Knapp, Alfred Averill. *Some of the Descendants of Robert and Jane McCune of Bourbon and Nicholas Counties, Kentucky.* Winter Park, FL, College Press, 1956. 57p. [D8413].

McCURDY -- McCurdy, Michael L. *A Compendium of Documents Pertaining to the McCurdy Family of Kentucky and Utah.* Silver Spring, MD, McCurdy, 1982. 49 leaves. [DS471].

McCURLEY -- McCurley, James Bernard, Jr. *Some American Ancestors of James Bernard McCurley, Jr. and Margaret Anne McCurley. Also DeHoff family.* rev. Louisville, KY, J. S. McCurley, 1983. 40 l. [C454; NG66].

McDONALD -- Williams, Mrs. Flora McDonald. *The Glengarry McDonalds of Virginia.* Louisville, KY, George C. Fetter Company, 1911. [VV].

McDANIEL -- Harris, Charles G. *McDaniel Family Record; Family of Stephen McDaniel, sr.,* Louisville, KY, Franklin Printing Co., 1929. 1, 5-179p. [L11015; D8422].

McDOWELL -- Green, Thomas Marshall. *Historic Families of Kentucky with Special Reference to Stocked Immediately Derived from the Valley of Virginia; Tracing in Detail the Various Genealogies and Connexions and Illustrating from Historical Sources Their Influence upon Political and Social Developments of Kentucky and the States of the South and West .. 1st Series.* Cincinnati, OH, 1889 or 1890. iv, 304p. [L11053].

McFADIN -- McFadin, Maude A. *The John Stephen McFadin Family of North Carolina, Kentucky, Indiana, and Kansas.* North Newton, KS, Mennonite Press, 1971. 111p. Includes memoirs of George E. McFadin. [NG66; D8462; X-FW/LA/NY/SP].

McFARLAND -- Campbell, Kathryn Hutcherson. *The McFarland Clan of North Carolina,*

Kentucky, Missouri. Dallas, Campbell, 1974. viii, 188 l. [D8464].

McFARLAND -- McFarland, Robert M. *Our McFarland Family in Early Kentucky and Since.* Atlanta, GA, R. M. McFarland, Jr., 1982. vi, 113p. [C457].

McGAVIN -- McGavic, Adrian Don. *McGuffock to McGaffick to McGavock, McGavic and McGavick: The Scotch-Irish-American Genealogy of the Families - 1st ed.* N. Fort Myers, FL, A. D. McGavic, 1988. Utica, KY, McDowell Publications, 576p. 1. McGavin family. 2. Scots-Irish-Genealogy. 3. Ireland-Genealogy. [G440].

McGLASSON -- Dye, B. R. E. *McGlasson Family in Virginia and Boone County, Kentucky.* Hebron, KY, 1972. 28, 5 leaves. [X-FW; VV].

McGREGOR -- McGregor, Howard Wayne. *McGregor History: The John Burse McGregor's Line in West Kentucky. Illustrated by Howard W. McGregor; Photographs by Fletcher Ashby, Jr.* Utica, KY, McDowell Publications, 1984. xiv, 232p. [C458].

McHARGUE -- McHargue, Barbara Sue. *History and Genealogy, History and Genealogy, the Family of McHargue in America.* Corbin, KY,Westbrook Printing Co., 1938. 2p., 58p. L lists family name as McHARG. [L11108; D8492].

McKEE -- Green, Woodford McKee. *Supplement to McKees of Virginia and Kentucky by George W. McKee.* NP, 1972-1975. 34 leaves. [D8517; VV].

McKEE -- McKee, George Wilson. *The McKees of Virginia and Kentucky.* Pittsburgh, PA, McKee, Press of J. B. Richards, 1891. 2, 3-196p. NG shows 199p. [L11154; NG67; D8518; VP; VV].

McKEE -- Mackey, Everette, Barbara M. Grider, Hazel Wells. *Founders of the Mackey Clan of*

Kentucky. Albany, KY, Gibson Print. Co., 1980. 28p. 1. McKee family. 2. Kentucky-Genealogy. C lists as MACKEY with n.d. [G442; C461].

McKEE -- Paris, Amy. [G442]. See above: CULLEN. [G168].

McKINNEY -- Gross, Dorothy P. *Reuben Harrison McKinney of Kentucky and Missouri, 1808-1881.* Edmonds, WA, D. P. Gross, 1989. 1 v. (various pagings). 1. McKinney family. 2. McKinney, Reuben Harrison, 1808-1881-Family. 3. Kentucky-Genealogy. 4. Missouri-Genealogy. [G443].

McKISSICK -- Burgner, Walter C. *McKissick - Kissick Family of Fleming County, Kentucky, Knox County, Indiana, (and) Allen County, Ohio.* Lima, OH, n.d. Various pagings. [X-FW].

McLAUGHLIN -- McLaughlin, Arthur Lee. *The McLaughlin Family History.* Owensboro, KY, McDowell Publications, 1980. 76 l. [C461].

McLEAN -- Trotter, Salley Stone (Mrs. W. C. Jr.). *McLean, The Family of Judge Alney and Tabitha McLean of Greenville, Kentucky.* Greenville, MS, Trotter Genealogy, 1983. 63p. 1 folded leaf of plates. [C462].

McMURTRIE -- LeBaron, Esther McMurtry. *William McMurtry of Kentucky and Alabama and His Descendants.* Largo, FL, 1971. vii, 128p. [S1679].

McMURTRIE -- McMurtry, Richard K. *McMurtrie; Ancestors and Descendants of Joseph McMurtrie (1764-1846) of New Jersey and Pennsylvania, Including the Arrival and Early History of the Family in America.* Lexington, KY, McMurtrie Clam Family Historical Record Worldwide, 1968. viii, 53 leaves. [S1678; VP].

McMURTRY -- LeBaron, Esther Murty. *William McMurtry of Kentucky and Alabama.* Austin, TX, 1977. ix, 142p. [D8560].

McMURTRY -- McMurtry, David C. *Report to the National Societies of the Daughters of the American Revolution and the Sons of the American Revolution on the Inaccuracies in the Family and Revolutionary War Service Records of John McMurtrie of Philadelphia, John McMurtrie of New Jersey and Tennesee, Captain John McMurtrie of Kentucky as Recorded by Frederick James McMurtrie.* Lexington, KY, McMurtry, 1983. 1 v. in various pagings. [DS482].

McMURTRY -- McMurtry, David Cornelius. *The McMurtry Family of Harrison County, Kentucky.* Lexington, KY, McMurtrie Clan-Family Historical Records Worldwide (The Alexander David McMurtrie Collection), 1971. vii, 115 l. [D8561].

McNABB -- Beman, M. E. *McNabbs in Kentucky, Indiana, Iowa.* Ames, IA, 196_. Unp. [X-FW].

McNEESE -- McNeese-McMenama, Henrietta. *McNeese - McNees Family History: "The Brothers Three," Jacob W., Joseph, Jehu and Their Descendants.* Lexington, KY, H. McNeese-McMenama, 1983. 364, 35p. [C463].

McQUISTON -- McQuiston, Leona Bean. *The McQuiston, McCuiston, and McQuesten Families, 1620-1937.* Louisville, KY, Standard Press, 1937. xx, 750p. D gives xiv, 750p. [L11276; D8589].

McROBERTS -- Mills, Harry Willard. *McRoberts Family; Some Notes on: McRoberts' in Pennsylvania, Virginia and Kentucky; McRoberts Family of Lincoln County, Ky. A Family History Miniature.* Washington, DC, 1943. [VV].

MEAD -- Prichard, A. M. *Mead Relations; Mead, Brown, Powell, Keyser, Kelly, Trumbo, Austin, Toler, Prichard. Virginia, Kentucky.* Staunton, VA, 1933. 3, 9-265p. [L11677; VV].

MEADOR -- Newton, Jane Meador. *Descendants of Ambrose Meador, Bedford County, Virginia,* *to Breckinridge County, Kentucky, 1733-1988.* Utica, KY, McDowell Publications, 1988. 240p. 1. Meador family. 2. Meador, Ambrose, ca. 1730-1795-Family. 3. Virginia-Genealogy. 4. Kentucky-Genealogy. [G447].

MEDARIS -- Cooley, Elizabeth Morrow. *The Medaris Family of Early Clermont Co., Ohio.* Fort Thomas, KY, 1957. 11 leaves. FW shows 9 pages. [NG70; X-FW].

MEREDITH -- Basham, Kay Joyce Yates. *The Meredith Family History of Edmonson County, Kentucky.* Louisville, KY, K. J. Y. Basham, 1984. 63 leaves. [C468].

MERRICK -- Myrick, Victor R. *Myrick Family History.* Owensboro, KY, McDowell Publs., 1980. 116p. 3 leaves of plates. [C469].

MERSHON -- Swiger, Loraine B. *History of Henri Marchand II Family in America with Descendants of Timothy Mershon, Sr., of Ohio.* Owensboro, KY, McDowell Publications, 1981. 210p. [C470].

MERIWETHER -- Meriwether, David. *The Descendants of Thomas Merriwether.* Louisville, KY, 1891, 8p. [X-LI].

MERSHON -- Swiger, Lorraine B. *A Supplement to the Mershon Book.* NP, L. B. Swiger, 1983. 67p. [C470].

MILBY -- Wright, Eunice Montgomery. *John Milby, 1825-1906, Children and Grandchildren; Drury Hudson Milby, 1845-1921 and His Descendants.* __, KY, E. M. Wright, 1980. 53 l. 1. Milby family. 2. Milby, John, 1825-1906-Family. 3. Kentucky-Genealogy. [G454].

MILLER -- Hyatt, Harry Middleton. *The Millers of Millersburg, Kentucky.* Vienna, VA?, A. Holzhaussen's Successors, 1929. x, 200p. [L11887].

MILLER -- Katz, Gertrude Morton Price. *Ansil Daniel Miller, 1872-1953, Charles Daniel*

Miller, 1889-1962, of Irvine and Richmond, Kentucky and Eustis, Florida and Their Families (Allied Families are Price, Bourne, Broaddus, Gentry, Daniel. NP, 196_ - . 29 leaves. [S1775].

MILLER -- McLaughlin, Arthur Lee. *The Miller Family History.* Owensboro, KY, McDowell Publications. 1980. ii, 20 leaves. [C474].

MILLER -- Miller, William Harris. *History and Genealogies of the Families of Miller, Woods, Harris, Wallace , Maupin, Oldham, Kavanaugh, and Brown, with Interspersions of the Families of Dabney, Reid, Martin, Broaddus, Gentry, Jarman, Jameson, Ballard, Mullins, Michie, Moberly, Covington, Browning, Duncan, Yancey...* Richmond, KY, Miller, 1907. 2, 3-728, 127p. [L11872; D8800].

MILLER -- Waterman, Marilyn Miller. *The James Millers of Adams County, Ohio.* Lexington, KY, Waterman Enterprises, 1984. 107 p., 7 leaves of plates. [C475].

MILLS -- Sparacio, Ruth Trickey and Sam. [G456]. See above: LINDSAY. [G403]

MILWARD -- Macdonald, Margaret Taylor. *The Milward Family of Lexington, Kentucky, 1803-1969.* Dallas, TX, 1970. 177p. [NG71].

MITCHELL -- Allen, Estill Franklin. *Cousins: Handbook and Family History of Mitchell, Allen, Gilleland, and Related Families from Virginia into Georgia, North Carolina, Kentucky, Tennessee, Missouri, Mississippi, Illinois, Iowa, Arkansas, Louisiana, Oklahoma, New Jersey, Texas, California, Florida, and Idaho, mid 1700's to 1980.* Brownwood, TX, Howard Payne University, 1981. xxiv, 347p. [C477; VV].

MITCHELL -- Fowke, Gerard. *Mitchell, Smith, Fowke of Maryland, Virginia, Kentucky.* NP, 1924. 442p. [X-FW; VV].

MIZE -- Miller, Franklin, Jr. *The Isaac Mize Family of Eastern Kentucky.* Gambier, OH, F. Miller, 1985. 396p. [C478; NG71; DC2588].

MONTAGUE -- Sparacio, Ruth Trickey and Sam. [G461]. See above: LINDSAY. [G403].

MONTGOMERY -- Larkin, Thomas E. *Montgomery Family in Colonial Charles County, Maryland and Descendants in Kentucky and in Indiana.* Mt. Pocono, PA, 1944. 55p. [X-FW].

MONTGOMERY -- Wright, Eunice Montgomery. *Montgomery Family Records.* Campbellsville, KY, E. M. Wright, 1979. 99 leaves. 1. Montgomery family. 2. Kentucky-Genealogy. [G462].

MOORE -- Schoene, Charles E. *The Moores of Virginia and Kentucky.* Belleair Bluffs, FL, Bessie I, Moore, 1974. vii, 208p. [S1788; D8947; VV].

MONET -- Money, Harold S. *James Money, Kentucky Pioneer: Descendants and Related Families: The Money Tree.* Utica, KY, McDowell Publications, 1983. xii, 232p., 12 pages of plates. [C480].

MOORE -- Moore, Marjorie W. *John Jameson Moore, 1819-1879 and Lucy Jane Yates, 1832-1896 of Kentucky, Indiana, Iowa and Their Descendants: Including a Brief Outline of Their Ancestors and Brothers' and Sisters' Families as Known.* Brooklyn, IA, M. W. Moore, 1983. 80p. [C484].

MORAN -- Wright, Eunice Montgomery. *The Thomas D. Moran Family.* Campbellsville, KY, E. M. Wright, 1984. 83 leaves. 1. Moran family. 2. Moran, Thomas D., b.1832-Family. 3. Kentucky-Genealogy. [G464].

MOREHEAD -- Jaques, Lola Herron. *Kentucky Families Descended From Charles and Mary (Turner) Moorehead.* NP, 1979. xxv, 192p. [D8959].

MORGAN -- Harris, Mayme E. F. *Morgan - Gray - Swank - Allied Families in Maryland, Pennsylvania, (and) Kentucky.* Chicago Heights, IL, Sauk Trail Chapter, D.A.R., 1970. 206P. [X-FW].

MORRIS -- Cunningham, Lelia Morris. *A Genealogy of William Morris the Patriot and Pioneer.* Wilmore, KY, Cunningham, 1969. 19, 10 l. [D8993].

MORRIS -- Mitchell, Eula Eunice Park. *C. C.'s Clan: Morris, Arms, Mitchell, and Related Families, Conway, Shucks, Brooks, Denton, Hazelip, Washburn, Basham, Smith.* Utica, KY, McDowell Publications, 1984. ca.200p. [C487].

MORRISON -- Morrison, Granville Price. *[History of a Branch of the Morrison Family Whose Progenitor Emigrated to America.] Morrison Genealogy: A History of the Branch of the Morrison Family.* Owensboro, KY, McDowell Publications, 1980. 112p. Reprint: Originally published: History of a Branch of the Morrison Family Whose Progenitor Emigrated to America. Charlestown, WV, Jarrett Publ. Co., 1928 with a new index. [C487].

MOSLEY -- Mosley, R. L. *Epitome of the History of the Moseley Family: Ancestry and Descendants of Lt. Robert Moseley of Virginia and Kentucky.* Winter Park, FL, College Press, 1979. 99 leaves. [C489; VV].

MOSES -- Moses, Richard Asberry. *Moses; A Record of the Moses Tribe of (Kentucky).* Emlyn, KY, 1965. 171p. [L12260].

MOSS -- Moss, T. C. *The David Moss Family; Warren and Granville Co., N.C. Green, Adair, Mercer, Boyle, Barren, Hart and Warren County, Ky. Williamson and Maury Co., Tenn. Mississippi.* Memphis, TN, Print by C. Johnson and Assocs., 1968. 79p. [L12274].

MULKEY -- Willoughby, Eliza Smith. *Lineage of Vance Smith (MacDonald), Bowling Green, Kentucky and John Hesron MacDonald,*

Springfield, Illinois. Bowling Green, KY, Selby E. Smith, 1929. 54p. [D9095].

MULLEN -- Justice, Marie R. *One Mullins Family*. Pikeville, KY, M. R. Justice, 175p., 5 leaves. of plates. [C493].

MULLICA -- Willoughby, Elizabeth S. *Lineage of Vance Smith (MacDonald), Bowling Green, Kentucky and John Hesron MacDonald, Springfield, Illinois, 1636-1929.* Bowling Green, KY, S. S. Smith, 1929. 54p. [X-FW].

MUNDELL -- Barry, Ruby M. *The Mundell (Mundle) Family; Descendants of James Mundell and His Wife, Margaret (Garrett) of New Castle County, Delaware, and Greene County, Pa. And the Migrations of the Children into Kentucky, Ohio, West Virginia and Other Western States.* Kansas City, MO, 1968. Pages not given. [X-FW/NY; VP].

MURPHY -- Haney, Lucille N. *Lineage of John Curren Nickel and Emma Golden Murphy.* Lexington, KY, L. N. Haney, 1987. 111 leaves, 15 leaves of plates. 1. Nichols family. 2. Murphy family. 3. Nickell, John Curren, 1889-1969-Family. 4. Nickell, Emma Golden Murphy, 1895- -Family. [G473].

MURROW -- Murrow, Charles Harland. *The Murrow Family of Virginia, Kentucky, Indiana, Iowa, and Kansas. Descendants of James Murrow... A Partial Genealogy, Compiled from 1910 to 1940.* Des Moines, IA, 1940. 22 l. [L12373; VV].

MYERS -- Seaman, Sallyann Jean. *John Nicholas Mayer and All Known Descendants.* Owensboro, KY, McDowell Publications, 1981. ii, 140p., 8 leaves of plates. [C497].

N

NAPIER -- Ernst, Katherine Jane Napier. *History of the Napier Family in America:*

Descendants of Corporal Patrick Napier... Louisville, KY, Napier, 1987. 44p. [DC2691].

NASH -- Nash, James Henry. [G476]. See above: HOLMES. [G327]

NAVE -- Jacobs, Gladys E. *Genealogy of the Nave Family.* Lancaster, KY, Jacobs, Kelly, 1947. 56p. [D9173].

NEIGHBOURS -- Mackoy, Harry Brent. *A Study in Heridity and Environment; Being a Historical and Genealogical Sketch of the Ancestors of Joseph Henry Assel, Formerly James Joseph Neighbours of Cincinnatti, Ohio.* Covington, KY, Mackoy, 1922. 94p. FW gives no date. [D9200; X-FW].

NEIGHBOURS -- Mackoy, Harry Brent. *A Study in Heridity and Environment; Being a Historical and Genealogical Sketch of the Ancestors of Joseph Henry Assel, Formerly James Joseph Neighbours of Cincinnatti, Ohio.* Cincinnati, OH, A. H. Pugh Print. Co., 1953. 94p. [X-CH].

NETTERVILLE -- Laroussini, Winona Netterville. *Netterville Family.* Lexington, KY, Horlacher, (Distribution), 1977. 139 l. [D9221].

NOBLE -- Knox, Joan Ritchey. [G484]. See above: CANBY: [G118].

NORRIS -- Josserand, Gertrude Cleghorn. *Kentucky Descendants of Thomas Norris of Maryland, 1630-1953.* Ann Arbor, MI, Edwards Brothers, 1953. 134p. [D9314].

NORTHCUTT -- Northcutt, Dolly. *The Northcutt Families of Kentucky.* Longview, TX, Morris Pub. Co., Northcutt, 1960. 215 l. [D9326].

NORTON -- Morton, David. *The Norton of Russellville, Ky.* NP, 1952. 83 l. Typescript of 1891 edition, printed by J. P. Lippincott Co., Philadelphia. [D9329].

NORVELL -- Foreman, Twylia Norvell. *The Norvell Family Journal.* Madisonville, KY, Foreman, 1990. 323p. [DC2744].

NOURSE -- Lyle, Maria Catherine Nourse. *James Nourse and His Descendants.* Lexington, KY, Transylvania Printing Co., 1897. 138p. [D9345].

NOVINGER -- McNamara, Elizabeth W. *The Novinger Family of Dlauphin Co., Pa. and Adain Co., Mo.* Fort Thomas, KY, Novinger, 1978. 28 leaves. [D9346; VP].

O

OATES -- Winebarger, William Lloyd. *Oates - Earle And Related Families.* Graham, KY, OE & R Pub., Inc. 1972. 207p. FW indicates abridged version, same pagination. [NG75; D9367; X-FW].

O'DANIEL -- O'Daniel, V. F. *Snatches of O'Daniel, Hamilton, and Allied Ancestry and History in Maryland and Kentucky.* Somerset, OH, Rosary Press, 1933. 101p. [L12700; D9377].

OLD -- Clarke, Peyton Neale. *Old King William Homes and Families, etc.* Louisville, KY, J. P. Morton, 1897. [VV].

ORMSBY -- Pierce, Albert E. *Ormsby Families of Louisville Kentucky.* Tulsa, OK, Pierce, 1968. 26 l. [D9447].

ORR -- Ostendorff, Paul J. *William Orr of Ireland, Pennsylvania, and Kentucky with His Descendants through His Son William Vernon Orr, from 1870, Pa. (Including Families of Pollard, Vinson, and Thompson).* West St. Paul, MN, 1971. 61 leaves. [S1866].

OSBORN -- Osborn, Donald Lewis. *Genealogy of Edward and Sarah (Burchett) Osborn of Floyd County, Kentucky.* Lee's Summit, MO, 1970. 12p. [L12858; NG76].

OVERSTREET -- Overstreet, Joseph S. *My Great Grandfathers, Samuel, Gabriel, and James Overstreet.* Crestwood, KY, J. S. Overstreet, 1985. 48 leaves. 1. Overstreet family. 2. Overstreet, James, 1736-1817-Family. 3. Kentucky-Genealogy. [G498].

OWEN -- Barr, Lockwood. *Owens - Grubbs and Allied Families of Virginia and Kentucky.* New York, NY, 1940. 52 l. [L12905; VV].

OWEN -- Barr, Lockwood. *Owens - Grubbs and Allied Families of Virginia and Kentucky.* New York, NY, 1942. 41 leaves. [L12907].

OWENS -- Owens, David Hatfield. *Owens Family of Virginia... and Kentucky...* Ann Arbor, MI, Owens, 1988. 74, 18 leaves. 1. Owen family. 2. Owens, John, 1660-1712-Family. 3. Kentucky-Genealogy. 3. Virginia-Genealogy. DC gives 93 leaves. in various foliations. [G498; DC2799].

OWENS -- Owens, Lewis M. *Our Kentucky Kinfolks: Owens, Hammond, Tarter, Cooper, Robertson, Hopper, Leach, Wade, & Some Related Families.* Lexington, KY, Owens, 1976. 169p. in various pagings. [C521].

P

PAGET -- Hammon, Stratton O. *The Paget Family of Virginia, Kentucky, and Indiana.* Louisville, KY, 1941. Geneal. Table. VV shows date of 1918. [L12938; VV].

PAINE -- Payne, E. S. *Outline of Payne Family of Virginia and Kentucky and Allied Families.* NP, 1971. 32p. [X-FW; VV].

PARIS -- Paris, Amy. [G502; C526]. See above: CULLEN. [G168].

PARK -- Gum, Nell Marshall (Park). *Park of Kentucky, 1747-1929; With Allied Families: Benton, Bolan, Campbell, Chenault, Clark, Cobb, Covington, Dillingham, Duncan, Elliott,*

Gum, Henderson, Hume, Jacobs, Keller, Kidwell, Rayburn, Scrivner, Wagers, Wilson. Frankfurt, KY, Gum, 1929. x, 148. xv p. [L13035; NG77; D9562].

PARK -- Mitchell, Eula Eunice Park. *A Chick and Kin Book: Park - Ross Families.* Owensboro, KY, Mitchell, 1983. 90p. [DC2815].

PARK -- Park, Evelyn Potter. *Allen Park, 1745-1805 of Rowan County, North Carolina and Madison County, Kentucky; Including Some of His Descendants and Allied Families.* Chandler, OK, WR Park, 1970. x, 300p. [A517].

PARVIN -- Parvin, Richard A. *A Genealogy of the Decendants of Thomas Parvin of Kentucky.* Woodland Hills, CA, R. H. Parvin, 1978. 82 leaves. [C529].

PATRICK -- Patrick, Wellington. *Names and Family of Patrick... Presented at... Salyersville, Ky.* NP, 1940. 45 leaves. [X-FW].

PATTERSON -- Bailey, Jack Dalton. [G506]. See above: DEVINE. [G187].

PATTERSON -- Smith, Ethel Marion. *An Informal History of Virginia-Kentucky Pattersons in Illinois, Their Forebears and Their Kin Including the Lewises of Llangollen.* Washington, DC, 1948. vi, 208 leaves. [L13147; VV].

PATTERSON -- Willis, Irene Patterson. *The Descendants of Joseph (Joslip) Patterson and Sarah (Sallie) Martin Patterson of Grayson County, Kentucky: Genealogy 1800-1905.* Utica, KY, McDowell Publications, 1985- . v. <1- >. 1. Patterson family. 2. Patterson, Joseph, b.1767-Family. 3. Kentucky-Genealogy. [G506].

PATTON -- NAS. *The Pattons.* NP, Kentucky, DAR, G.R.C. 1938. 89 leaves. [D9671].

PEARCE -- Pearce, Marvin J. *Pearce Pioneers in Kentucky.* El Cerrito, CA, Pearce, 1969. 179p. [D9702].

PEARCE -- Pearce, Marvin J. *Pearce Pioneers in Kentucky. Supplement No. 1.* El Cerrito, CA, 9(sic), 1972. Paged 11 A - 15 B. [X-DP/SL/SP].

PEASE -- Rice, Philip J. *Pease Family History.* Monticello, KY, Manor Pub. Co., 1982. iv, 373, 18p. Cover Title: A Genealogical and Historical Record of the Descendants of John and Robert Pease. C gives iv, 373p. [C533; DC2849].

PEDDICORD -- Logan, Mrs. India W. P. *Kelion Franklin Peddicord of Quirk's Scouts, Morgan's Kentucky Cavalry, C.S.A. Biographical and Autobiographical, Together with a General Biographical Outline of the Peddicord Family.* New York and Washington, The Neale Publ. Co., 1908. 170p. [L13229].

PEDEN -- Peden, Henry C. *The Pedens of Southwest Virginia and Southcentral Kentucky, Descendants of John Peden (1734-1815) and Mary Smith (1734-1800).* Edgewood, MD, Peden, 1978. 126p. [C534; VV].

PEDEN -- Peden, Henry C. *The Pedens of Southwest Virginia and Southcentral Kentucky, Descendants of John Peden (1734-1815) and Mary Smith (1734-1806).* Baltimore, MD, Jet Printing Service, 1978. [DC2851].

PEDEN -- Peden, Henry C. *Genealogy of the Pedens of Kentucky, 1756-1986.* Bel Air, MD, 1986. viii, 415p. 1. Peden family. 2. Kentucky-Genealogy. [G509].

PEEBLES -- Whitley, Edythe R. *Peebles Family of Virginia, North Carolina, Kentucky, Illinois, Missouri, etc.* Seattle, WA, n.d. 50p. [X-SP; VV].

PELL -- Pell, Edna S. *The History and Descendants of John Pell and Nancy Harrison*

Pell of Fairfax County, Virginia, (through) 1989. Benton KY, E. S. Pell, Newark, OH, G. Sewell. 1990. iii, 271p. 1. Pell family. 2. Pell, John, ca.1765-1810-Family. [G509].

PERRY -- Hayes, Mrs. D. G. *Perry Family of Virginia and Kentucky.* NP, 1970. 29 l. [D9821; VV].

PETER -- McDonald, Frank V. *Supplement No. 1 to Edition B of the MacDonald Genealogy; Containing Records of the Descendants of Jesse Peter, One of the Pioneer Settlers near Mackville, Washington County, Kentucky; Together with a few Remarks on the Early History of the Peter Family.* Cambridge, MA, John Wilson & Son, University Press, 1880. 72p. NG shows as "Supplement No.1; Descendants of Jesse Peter of Washington County, Kentucky." [NG66; D9833].

PETERS -- Peters, Okey Erwin. *Conrad Peters and Wife Clara Snidow.* Paducah, KY, Paducah Printing Co., 1948. 229p. [D9842].

PETTY -- Mitchell, Eula Eunice Park. *A Chick and Kin Book.* Owensboro, KY, McDowell Publications, 1981-<1983 >. v. <1-4 > Vol 4 published in Utica, KY. V. 1. Petty-Gentry Families. -- V. 2. Bean - Boswell - Duke - Acton Families. -- V. 3. Thomas - Thomas Families. -- V. 4. Park - Ross Families. [C540].

PETTY -- Petty, Gerald M. *Petty, of England & Virginia; Wright of Virginia, Kentucky & Missouri; Riley of Maryland, Kentucky & Missouri; and Related Alexander, Copeland, Dale, Douglass, Givens, Hubbard, McClung, Owens, Patton, Paxton, Rowland, & Tedford Families.* Columbus, OH, 1973. [VV].

PETWAY -- Petway, Melva Koerner. *Petway's of America, 1600ca to 1990.* Benton, KY, M. K. Petway, 1990. 279, a-l p., 16p. of plates. 1. Petway family. 2. Edwards, Sara Petway. [G515].

PHELPS -- Roy, Nancy R. *The Phelps Family of Virginia and Kentucky and Allied Families.* La Mesa, CA, Roy, 1960. 166p. [D9882; VV].

PHILLIPS -- Rush, Peggy Francis. *The Phillips family of Station Run and Hardin's Creek, Washington County, Kentucky.* Minnetonka, MN, P. F. Rush, 1988. iii, 114p. 1. Phillips family. 2. Kentucky-Genealogy. [G517].

PHILPOT -- Bowling, Noland Hubbard. *Meet Your Ancestors: Some Ancestors of Edward Philpott (1599-1678)...* Utica, KY, McDowell, 1985. 389p. [DC2896].

PHILPOTT -- Bowling, Noland Hubbard. [G517]. See above: BARTON. [G38].

PHIPPS -- Young, Asher Leon. *The Phipps Tree.* Nashville, TN, A. L. Young, 1983. iii, 316p. "An expansion and updating of the Chapter that was in my book "Washington Young of Wayne County, Kentucky and his descendants, written in 1976". [C544].

PHIPPS -- Young, Asher Leon. *The Phipps Tree II: A Supplement to The Phipps Tree.* Nashville, TN, A. L. Young, 1989. iii, 332p. 1. Phipps family. 2. Kentucky-Genealogy. [G518].

PICKETT -- NAS. *Bibliography of Doctor Thomas Edward Pickett of Mysville, Kentucky.* Kentucky Historical Society, Frankfort, 1914. 16p. [L13592].

PIERCE -- Clore, Dorothy P. *Five Little Pierces in the Parsonage.* ___, KY, D. P. Clore, 1985. 311 leaves., 2 leaves of plates, 1. Pierce family. 2. Kentucky-Genealogy. [G518].

PIERCE -- Pearce, Marion J. Sr. *Pearce Pioneers in Kentucky with Notes on Related Families: Akin, Anderson, Arras, Benedict,*

Carroll, Gilbertz, Hoepfinger, Jordon, Ligon, Majors, Moss, Redmond, Stanhope, Stapleton, Swafford, Tipton, Torr. El Cerito, CA, 1969. 180p. [L13608].

PINKSTAFF -- Pinkstaff, Burton L. *The Pinkstaff Family.* Bowling Green, KY, Pinkstaff, 1982. 139p. [DS556].

PIRTLE -- Johnson, Henry M. and Henry J. Tilford. *The Family of John and Amelia Fitzpatrick Pirtle, Another Family of Distinction from the Lincoln County of Kentucky, Showing the Paternal Heirs as of January Nineteen thirty-five of Major John B. Pirtle Tracing from His Grandparents Rev. John Pirtle and Amelia Fitzpatrick Pirtle of Kentucky.* Louisville, KY, Gibbs-Inman Co., Inc., 1936. 80p. [L13646].

PLEASANTS -- Edmiston, Carroll Evan. *Our Families from the Atlantic Coast Colonies of 1665 to the California Pacific of 1974.* Danville, KY, 1974. 156p. [S1967].

PLUMMER -- Britt, Daniel S. [G522]. See above: BRITT. [G89].

POAGE -- Townsend, Catherine Poage. *The Poage Family of Kentucky and Virginia.* NP, 1939, 46 l. [D10014: VV].

POLK -- Patterson, Ruth Polk. *The Seed of Sally Good'n: A Black Family of Arkansas, 1833-1953.* Lexington, KY, University Press of Kentucky, 1985. xv, 183 p., 8 pages of plates. 1. Polk family. 2. Afro-Americans-Arkansas-Biography. 3. Arkansas-Biography. [G524; C550].

POLK -- Polk, James. *Last Labors of an Old Pioneer... Kentucky and Indiana.* NP, 1886. 83 leaves. [X-FW].

POLK -- Polk, William Harrison. *Polk Family and Kinsmen.* Louisville, KY, Bradley & Gilbert, 1912. 1, vii-xxvii, 742p. [L13712; D10024].

PONDER -- Saupe, Patricia. *Kentucky Ponders.* Moores Hill, IN, P. Saupe, 1983. xi, 878p. Updated by Kentucky Ponders Supplement (641p). 1988 1. Ponder family. [G525].

POPE -- White, Emery H. [G525]. See above: MAXEY. [G431].

PORTER -- Hinshilwood, Charles M. *The Descendants of William and Mary (Cathers) Porter, Who Settled on Big Raccoon Creek in Knox (now Lowell) County, Kentucky in the Year 1805.* South Pasedena, CA, 1976. 222p. [X-LA].

PORTER -- Lloyd, Emma Rouse. *Porter Family of Kentucky.* NP, nd, (Available for Consultation at the Lloyd Library, 309 West Court St., Cincinnati, OH.) [L13784].

PORTER -- Martin, Harry G. *Pickin Up The Porters.* Richmond, KY, Martin, 1983. 432p. [DS563].

PORTER -- Porter, William L. *List of Porter Families in the United States at the Time of the Taking of the 1790 Census.* Kansas City, MO, n.d. 19p. [X-FW].

POSEY -- Brown, Ethel Claire Posey Anderson. *God's Everlasting Bouquet of Poseys: Autobiography.* Bowling Green, KY, E. C. P. A. Brown, 1984. A-M, 198 leaves. [C553].

POWELL -- Potts, Merna P. *Powell Family Records... Descendants of Thomas Powell Sr., (1755-1813) and Nancy Chaney, Early Pioneers of Nicholas County, Ky.* Albany, OR, 1966. 54 leaves. [X-GF/SP].

POWELL -- Powell, Omegene Powers. [G528]. See above: BASHAM. [G38].

POWERS -- Powell, Omegene Powers. [G528]. See above; BENFIELD. [G48].

PRATHER -- Jennings, Kathleen. *Louisville's First Families; A Series of Genealogical*

Sketches... with Drawings by Eugenia Johnson. Louisville, KY, The Standard Printing Co., 1920. 176p. Contains the Bullitt, Prather, Clark, Churchill, Pope, Speed, Joyes, Veech, Thompson, Taylor, Bate, and Floyd Families. [L13846].

PRESTON -- Brown, Orlando. *Memoranda of the Preston Family.* Frankfort, KY, S. I. M. Major, 1842. 10p. [X-LI/SU].

PRESTON -- Brown, John Mason. *Memoranda of the Preston Family.* Frankfort, KY, S. I. M. Major, 1870. 64p. [X-FW/LI/MH].

PRESTON -- Dorman, John Frederick. *The Prestons of Smithfield and Greenfield in Virginia, Descendants of John and Elizabeth (Patton,) Preston Through Five Generations.* Louisville, KY, Filson Club, 1982. xiii, 441p., 11 l. of plates. [C557; NG81; DS564].

PRICE -- NAS. *Obituaries of Morton M. (Moses) Price, 1805-1876, and Wife, Frances (Fannie) Crosthwaite, 1822-1922, of Irvine, Estill County, Kentucky.* NP, 1971. 6 l. [S2003].

PRICE -- Katz, Gertrude Morton Price (Mrs. Alexander Katz). *The Kentuckians, Family History of Zachary Taylor Price, 1847-1912, and Wife, Amelia Farley, 1853-1939.* NP, 1971. 2 v. [S2004].

PRICE -- Katz, Gertrude M. P. *Index: Descendants of Colonel John Price (1757-1822) and Wife, Sarah Bourne, of Va. and Ky.* Tampa, FL, 1974. Various pagings. [X-FW].

PRICHARD -- Johnson, Martha Coleman. *The Prichard (Pritchard) Family; History and Genealogy of the Descendants of James and Eley Hughes Prichard of New Castle, Kentucky.* NP. 1915. 3, 5-230p. [L13922].

PRUITT -- Prewitt, Richard A. *Isham Prewitt of Virginia.* Grimes, IA, R. W. Prewitt, 1979. 125p. 1. Pruitt family. 2. Prewitt, Isham, ca.1725-1806-Family. 3. Virginia-Genealogy. 4. Kentucky-Genealogy. [G533].

PRYOR -- Harris, Hugh Henry. *The Pryor, Boyett & Jordan Families with Related Families.* Owensboro, KY, McDowell Publications, 1980. 163p. [C561].

PUCKETT -- Garrett, Hester Elizabeth. *Pucketts and Their Kin of Virginia, Kentucky, and Other Southern States.* Lansing, MI, Garrett, 1960. 285p. [D10211; VV].

PURDOM -- Bottom, Mabel Kirkland. *Marcus Purdom and His Descendants.* Harrodsburg, KY, Bottom, 1987. 55 leaves. [DC2974].

PUTNAM -- Putnam, Thomas Russell. *Putnam Genealogical Chart from 16th Century until 20th Century, Tracing the Descendants of the Early Virginia, Kentucky, Carolina Putnams, Who are Descended from Thomas Putnam, Who Landed in Virginia 1647 from England...* NP, 1938. Genealogical Table. [L14008].

PUTNAM -- Putnam, Thomas Russell. *Putnam Genealogy (Recording the Descendants of Thomas Putnam, the Immigrant to Virginia 1647) - Also an Enumeration of the Living Descendants of the "Virginia-Carolina-Kentucky" Putnams; Also Brief Genealogies of the Harper, Grover, and McGlasson Families.* Okmulgee, OK, 1938. 107p. [L14009; VV].

Q

QUAINTANCE -- Quaintance, Alfred M. *Genealogy of the Quaintance Family in Virginia and Kentucky.* Englewood, CO, Quaintance, 1968. vii, 73, 8 l. [D10245: VV].

QUEEN -- Dyer, Paul E. *John Queen (ca. 1720-1802/1805) of Loudon County, Virginia and Descendants, Mainly of Wayne County, West Virginia (early Cabell) and Eastern Kentucky.* Louisville, KY, Dyer, 1980. 602p. [C564; VV].

QUIER -- Gerlach, Mary Ruth Jackson. *Descendants of Quier Family - 2nd ed.* - Louisville, KY, Laser Graphics, 1990. 440p. [G538].

QUINTON -- Schermerhorn, Sharon Minor. [G539]. See above: ANDERSON. [G13].

QUISENBERRY -- Fox, Martha Stuart. *Stuart, Quisenberry: Kith and Kin.* Winchester, KY, M. S. Fox, 1986. v, 270p., 1 p. of plates. 1. Stuart family. 2. Quisenberry family. [G539].

R

RADCLIFFE -- NAS. *American Radcliffes: Carolina, Kentucky, Pennsylvania Branch.* NP, 1963. 2 Genealogical Tables. [L14053].

RADCLIFFE -- Radcliffe, Edward J. *Carolina - Kentucky - Pennsylvania Radcliffes. A Genealogical Record.* NP, n.d. 6p. (folder). [X-PH].

RAINEY -- Chaney, Roselind Rainey. *The Rainey Family: Descended from John Raney of Clark County, Kentucky.* Greenwoood, IN, R. R. Chaney, 1984. iv, 64p. 1. Rainey family. 2. Raney, d. ca. 1820-Family [G541; C567].

RALEIGH -- Railey, William Edward. *History of the "Raileys and Kindred Families".* Ann Arbor, MI, University Microfilms International, 1979. 147p. Running Title: The Randolphs and Their Railey Connections. Written for Kentucky historical magazine the Register, 1911-1918. Reprint of the 1922 ed. published in Frankfurt, KY. C lists as RALEY. [G541; C568].

RALPH -- Holbrook, Alberta Ralph. *The Ralph Family History, 1770-1979.* Hartford, KY, McDowell Publications, 1979. iv, 34p., 2 leaves of plates. [C568].

RALPH -- Ralph, Anita Belle (Shawn). *A History of the Genealogy of the Ralph Family* *from England to America, to Their Settlement in Kentucky up to the Present Time, 1734-1982.* Utica, KY, McDowell Publications, 1982. A-H leaves, 200p. [C568].

RAMEY -- Minix, Myrtle Jayne Wheeler. *Remy - Ramey Record and Preservation of Our Ancestors and Their Descendants, 1654-1981.* Ashland, KY, M. J. W. Minix, 1982. 249 l. [C568].

RANDOLPH -- Railey, William E. *Brief Sketches of the Randolphs and Their Connections: The Woodsons, the Keiths, the Strothers, the Plesants, and the Mayos. Also, a Brief Sketch of the Owsleys, and the Whitleys.* Frankfurt, KY, Robert Prtg. Co., 1929. 160p. [X-LI/NY].

RANSOM -- Ransom, Robert G. *The Ransom Family of Western Kentucky: A History and Genealogy.* Murfreesboro, TN, Ransom, 1977. vii, 386p. [C570].

RAPIER -- Donnelly, Mary Louise. *Rapier, Hayden and Allied Families, Colonial Maryland and Kentucky. Wifried Vollmer Illustrator.* Burke, VA, M. L. Donnelly, 1978. v, 579p., 1 page of plates. [C570].

RAY -- Franklin, Della P. *Ray Connections.* Cookeville, TN, D. P. Franklin, 1990. iv, 459, 60p. 1. Ray family. 2. Tennessee-Genealogy. 3. Kentucky-Genealogy. [G544].

RAY -- McDaniel, Marcella Marie. *Life and History of James Homer Ray and His Descendants.* Owensboro, KY, McDowell Publications, 1980 or 1981. 126p., 34 pages of plates. [C572].

RECTOR -- Smart, Clarissa Ruth Barnes. *The Rectors of Wayne County, Kentucky.* Charlottesville, Wayside, 1975. 336 leaves. [DC3031].

REDFERN -- Babbitt, Golden Hughes. *More About the Redfearns and Their Descendants.*

Utica, KY, Babbitt, 1978. vii, 46p. 4 leaves of plates. [C573].

REED -- Bryant, Mary Reed. *The James Robert Reed Family Tree.* Utica, KY, McDowell Publications, 1982. 84p., 2 p. of plates. [C574].

REED -- McCubbin, Gleason M. *Eli Read / Reed Descendants.* Elizabethtown, KY, G. M. McCubbin, 1983. 686p. [C574].

REEVES -- Bacus, Elizabeth R. *Reeves Family of Missouri, (by way of England, Virginia, Kentucky, Ohio and Indiana.)* NP, nd, 7, 4p., 5 leaves. [X-FW; VV].

RENFREW -- Mallisee, Natalia Decker. *The John Renfrow Family in Grayson County: History and Genealogy.* Leitchfield, KY, N. D. Mallisee, 1983. 161p. 1. Renfrew family. 2. Renfrow, John, ca.1780-ca.1799-Family. 3. Kentucky-Genealogy. [G549].

RENICK -- Ardery, Julia Hoge (Spencer). *Renick - Morris Ancestral Chart Compiled by Gertrude Trimble (Renick) Bell, Wife of James Duncan Bell... Drawn by Bayless Harden.* Frankfort, KY, 1944. Genealogical. Table. [L14252].

REYNOLDS -- Reynolds, William Clark. *Diary of William Clark Reynolds, 1860-1863.* Florence, KY, Wm. & Anne Fitzgerald, 1956. 21p. [X-FW].

RICE -- Rice, John Haden. *History of the Aukers, Conly, Rice, Stambaugh & Witten Families of Johnson Co., Kentucky.* Baltimore, MD, Gateway Press, 1976. 391p., 1 leaf of plates. [C580].

RICHARDS -- Richards, Elvin. *Descendants of George Richards and Catherine Bush: Family History.* Belpre, OH, Richards, 1978. 86p. [C581].

RICHARDSON -- Brown, Frances Rountree. *Richardson History and Genealogy.* Cave City, KY, Brown, 1986. 501p. [DC3073].

RICHARDSON -- Colby, Mary E. *The Richardson Family, Pioneers of Oregon and Utah; An Account of the Descendants of Shadrack and Betsy Richardson of Kentucky Compiled From Family Traditions and Records Covering the Migration of the Members from Kentucky to Illinois, Iowa, Oregon, and Utah.* Dallas, Polk Co., OR, Printed by the Itemizer-Observer, 1940. 39p. [L14354].

RICHARDSON -- Rouse, Mrs. Robert M. *The Lemuel Richardson Family.* Ft. Mitchell, KY, Rouse, 1972. 7, 18 leaves. [D10507].

RICHARDSON -- Rouse, Nancy E. (Mrs. Robert M.) *The Lemuel Richardson Family, 1773-1983.* Ft. Mitchell, KY, Estate of Mrs. Robert M. Rouse, 1983. 99, 22 leaves. [C581; D10507].

RICKETTS -- Davis, W. E. *The Records Lineage: John, John, Jr., Josiah, Spencer Alexander, John, etc.* W. E. Davis, Glendale, OH, 1985. 1 v. (various foliations). 1. Ricketts family. 2. Kentucky-Genealogy. [G554].

RINEY -- Webber, Patricia R. *Riney Family, Maryland, Kentucky, Missouri.* Nashville, TN, Webber, 1977. ix, 173p. [C584].

RINGO -- NAS. *Ringo Reunion in Print.* Covington, KY, 1934- v. 1- Oct 1934- . [L14416].

RINGO -- NAS. *Ringo Family History Series.* Alhambra, CA, The Freeborn Family Organization, 1980. _ v. Vol. 13 is Series Index. Vol 2 Written by David Leer Ringo. [DC3089].

RINGO -- NAS . *The Ringo Family History Series.* Alhambra, CA, Freeborn Family Organization, 1980-1986. 13 v. in 10. 1.

Ringo family-collected works. NGS shows 13 v. in 9. [G557; NGS10].

RINGO -- NAS. *The Ringo Family History Series.* Alhambra, CA, Freeborn Family Organization, 1980-<1984. >. <v. 2-13 in 8 > [C585].

RINGO -- NAS. *The Ringo Family History Series.* Alhambra, CA, Freeborn Family Organization, 1980-1982. 9 v. in 5. [DS602].

RINGO -- King, May Ringo. *Ringo Researcher.* Eugene, OR, King, 1985-. _ v. Quarterly. See DAR Shelflist for Library Holdings. [DC3090].

RINGO -- Ringo, David Leer. *The Ringos in Europe.* Alhambra, CA, Freeborn Family Organization, 1984-1986. 2v. (xvii, 652p.) NGS shows v. 1. 652p. 1. Ringo family. 2. France-Genealogy. 3. Belgium-Genealogy. 4. Netherlands-Genealogy. [G557; NGS10].

RINGO -- Ringo, David Leer. *The First Five Generations of the Ringo Family In America: including as a supplement, Early Collateral Families, by May Ringo King.* Alhambra, CA, 1982. v.2. 388p. [C585; NGS10].

RINGO -- NAS. *The Line of Descent From Phillip Ringo (1D2B1): b.1750, Hunterdon Co., NJ. d.1785, Loudon Co., VA. The Line of Descent from Cornelius Ringo (1D2B3) b.1753, Hunterdon Co., NJ, d.1836, Henry Co., KY.* Alhambra, CA, Freeborn Family Organization, 1981. v.3-4. v, 110, vi, 158p. [C585; NGS10].

RINGO -- NAS. *The Line of Descent From Major Ringo (1D2B4) b.1755, Hunterdon Co., NJ d.1838, Montgomery Co., KY (with a diary of Mrs. Mary Ringo). The Line of Descent From John Ringo (1D2B5) b.1758, Hunterdon Co., NJ, d.1829.* Alhambra, CA, Freeborn Family Organization, 1981. v.5-6. vi, 112, vi, 111. [C585; NGS10].

RINGO -- NAS. *The Line of Descent From Samuel Ringo (1D2B6) b.1761, Hunterdon Co., NJ, d.1827, Ray Co., MO. The Line of Descent From Joseph Ringo (1D2B7) b.1763, Hunterdon Co., NJ, d.1852, Montgomery Co., KY.* Alhambra, Freeborn Family Organization, CA, 1980. v.7-8. vi, 97; vi, 171p. [C585; NGS10].

RINGO -- NAS. *The Line of Descent From John Ringo (1D2E1) b.1761, Hunterdon Co., NJ, d.1843, Spencer Co., KY. The Line of Descent From Alburtis (Burtis) Ringo (1D2ED2) b.1763, Hunterdon Co., NJ, d.1852, Fleming Co., KY.* Alhambra, CA, Freeborn Family Organization, 1981. v.9-10. vi, 108, vi, 165p. [C584; NGS10].

RINGO -- NAS. *A Documentary History of the Ringo Family in America.* Alhambra, CA, Freeborn Family Organization. 1982. v. 11, vii, 342p. [C584; NGS10: DS601].

RINGO -- NAS. *Ringo Family Update: Including Corrections, Up-date and Pictures for Volumes 2 Thru 11.* Alhambra, CA, Freeborn Family Organization, 1983. v.12. x, 328p. [C585; NGS10].

RINGO -- NAS. *Family Name Index: Ringo Family Volumes II Thru XII.* Alhambra, CA, Freeborn Family Organization 1984. v.13. ix, 378p. [C585; NGS10].

RINGGOLD -- Veazey, Duncan. *Ringgold of Kent and Queen Anne's Counties, Maryland.* Louisville, KY, John P. Morton, 1900. 19p. [X-FW].

RIONS -- McCann, Wm. R. *Short Genealogy of Rions and Ruckers: Connecting These Families in Kentucky with Their Virginia Forebears.* NP, 1959. [VV].

RITCHIE -- Ritchie, Jean. *Singing Family of the Cumberlands.* Lexington, KY, University Press of Kentucky, 1988. vi, 258p. Originally published New York, Oxford University Press,

1955. 1. Ritchie, Jean. 2. Folk singers-Applachian Region-Biography. 3. Ritchie family. 4. Folk music-Applachian Region. 5. Folk songs, English-Applachian Region. [G558].

ROBERTS -- Calhoun, Logan E. [G560]. See above: CALHOUN. [G115].

ROBERTS -- Cash, Ben LeGrande. [G560]. See above: ELMORE. [G213].

ROBERTS -- Clay, Grady. *The Roberts - Solomon Family Geography, Macon Georgia, 1826-1987...* Louisville, KY, G. Clay, 1987. iii, 39p. 1. Roberts family. 2. Solomon family. 3. Dwellings-Georgia-Macon. 4. Macon (Ga.)-Geography. [G560].

ROBERTS -- Fowler, Ila Earle. *The Roberts Family of Robertstown, Caldwell County, Kentucky.* NP, 1946. 1 v. (various foliations). [D10580].

ROBERTSON -- Ball, Helen A. *Richard David and Eliza Ann Alloway Robertson: Their Ancestors and Descendants, Virginia, Kentucky, Missouri.* East Lansing, MI, 1979. [VV].

ROBINSON -- Beach, T. J. *Robinson Family History: A History of the Ancestors and Descendants of Noel and Martha Arnold Robinson of Gallatin County, Kentucky.* Kansas City, MO, T. J. Beach, 1982. 177, xvii p. Title: The Noel Robinson Family. 1. Robinson family. 2. Kentucky-Genealogy. [G561; C588].

ROBINSON -- Beach, T. J. *Robinson Family History: A History of the Ancestors and Descendants of Noel and Martha Arnold Robinson of Gallatin County, Kentucky. -- Rev. --* Weston, MO, T. J. Beach, 1985. 173, xxi p. Title: The Noel Robinson Family. 1. Robinson family. 2. Kentucky-Genealogy. [G561; C588].

ROBINSON -- Robinson, Richard A. *Family Records of Lyles Robert and Catherine Worthington Robinson (who resided near*

Winchester, Va.) and Their Descendants. Louisville, KY, Brewers Print., 1985. 3-125p. [X-FW/LI/MH; VV].

ROCHESTER -- Strange, Agatha Rochester. *House of Rochester in Kentucky.* Harrodsburg, KY, Democrat Printing Co., 1889. 128p. NG shows 129p. [NG; D10652; X-FW/LI/NY].

ROGERS -- Rogers, Ellen Stanley & Diane. *Rogers and Related Families of Estill County, Kentucky.* Irvine County, KY, E. Rogers, Stanton, KY, D. Rogers, 1980. iv, 362p. [C592].

ROGERS -- Rogers, Hopewell L. *Rogers.* Louisville, KY, Rogers, 1940. 71, 48p. [D10697].

ROGERS -- Rogers, Warren T. *Descendants of Nathaniel Rogers Who Came to Kentucky in 1801.* St. Paul, MN, 1944. 8 folded genealogical charts in binder. [X-MH].

ROGERS -- Van Valin, Minnie D. *Aquilla Wayne Rogers, Revolutionary Patriot of Pennsylvania, Kentucky, and Indiana.* NP, 1941. 261 leaves. [D10703; VP].

ROGERS -- Williamson, Mamie. *Lineage of Mary Frances Rogers (Mamie) Williamson.* Florence, KY, W. and A. Fitzgerald, 1954. 6 leaves. CH & FW show Unpaged. [DS612; X-CH/FW].

ROGERS -- Williamson, Mamie and Fitzgerald, William and Anne. *History of the Rogers Family.* Florence, KY, 1958. 63 leaves. [NG84].

ROGERS -- Williamson, Mary F. R. *History of the Rogers Family.* Florence, KY, 1958. 51 leaves. [X-CH/FW].

ROLLINS -- Barnard, Josephine R. T. *Partial Family Record of the Descendants of Lee and Susan Penn Rollins, Who Emigrated from Bourbon*

County, Ky. to Clay County, Mo. in the Fall of 1830. NP, 1930. 64p. [X-FW].

ROSE -- Rose, Christine. *(The) Brothers: Capt. Lewis, Matthias and Martin Rose, Sons of Gottlieb/Godlove Rose of Va., Pa., Ky., Ind., and Mo.* San Jose, CA, Rose Family Bulletin, 1972. 55p. [X-FW].

ROSS -- Heggs, Esther M. *Ross Family of Scotland, Virginia, Kentucky, Missouri, Iowa, Texas.* NP, nd, 64p. [X-FW; VV].

ROUSE -- Lloyd, Emma Rouse. *Rouse Family of Virginia and Kentucky.* NP, n.d. Pages not given. (Available for Consultation at the Lloyd Library, 309 West Court St., Cincinnati, OH.) [L14742; VV].

ROWAN -- Capps, Randall. *The Rowan Story: From Federal Hill to My Old Kentucky Home. -- Limited 1st ed.* -- Bowling Green, KY, Homestead Press, 1976. xi, 110p., 4 leaves. of plates. 1. Rowan family. 2. Bardstown (Ky.)-Genealogy. 3. Federal Hill (Bardstown, Ky.) [G571; C600; X-NY].

ROWAN -- Allison, Young E. *The Old Kentucky Home Immortalized by Stephen C. Foster; its Song and Story.* Federal Hill, Bardstown, KY, 1923. 40p. [L14752].

ROWE -- Adkins, Clara Pauline. *Genealogy of the Rowes of Virginia and West Virginia and Connecting Families (1697 to 1977).* Fort Gay, KY, 1977. 126p., 9 leaves of plates. [C600; VV].

ROWE -- Brooks, Patricia Ann. *History of the Families: Rowe, Snell, Casebier, Hines, Bozeman, Rone, Greer, and France.* Utica, KY, McDowell Publications, 1984. iv, 185p. [C600].

ROWLAND -- Sheridan, Richard C. *Richardson Rowland (1791-1872) and His Family... Tennessee and Kentucky.* Sheffield, AL, Sheridan, 1975. 47p. [X-DP].

ROY -- Roy, Nancy Reba. *The Roy Family of Virginia and Kentucky.* Fellows, CA, Roy, 1935. 190p. [L14763; D10803; VV].

ROY -- Roy, Nancy R. *Early Records of the Roy Family of Virginia and Kentucky.* La Mesa, CA, 1963. 12 leaves. [X-LA; VV].

ROYCE -- Patton, Mary Royce. *Royce and Gillespie Family Book.* Ft. Thomas, KY, Patton, 1962. 75p. [D10806; X-FW].

RUBY -- Ruby, Jay W. & Ruth. *History of the Rubi - Ruby Family of Switzerland and America.* Utica, KY, McDowell, 1987. v, 250p. [DC3174].

RUCHTI -- Brady, Mary Ann Ward. *Ruchti, Deppen, Yeakley , Stonebreaker, Fruits, Newkirk, Ward Genealogy and Family History.* Utica, KY, McDowell Publications, 1982. iii, 190p. [C601].

RUDOLPH -- Rudolph, Frances L. W. *Descendants of Rechel Rudolph, Robert Reuben Rudolph, John and Elizabeth Chism, Isaac Hust, Thomas F. Woods, Alexander Black, sr. Stokes Family. Descendants of Andrew J. Rudolph. Dakins and Faulkners. Descendants of Arthur Johnson, William Hosick, and Thomas and Moon Families of Kentucky.* Washington, DC, 1948. 2, 3, 109 leaves. Includes "Sources of Information". [X-FW/NY].

RUNYON -- Runyon, Robert and Amos. *Runyon Genealogy; A Genealogy of the Runyon Families Who Settled Early in Kentucky, North Carolina, Virginia and West Virginia.* Brownsville, TX, 1955. 194p. [L14811; VV].

RUSH -- Gorman, Dorothy Dowden. *History and Genealogy of the Rush Family; In Particular One Line on the Descendants of John Rush, the Third Son and Fifth Issue of the Emigrant Captian John Rush.* Louisville, KY, 1977. 20p. [NG86].

RUSSELL -- Des Cognets, Anna Russell. *William Russell and His Descendants.* Lexington, KY, S. F. Wilson, 1884. 4, 124p. [L14837].

RYAN -- Ryan, Perry T. *The Ryan Family of Breckenridge County, Kentucky.* ___, KY, P. T. Ryan, 1983. ca.450p. [C605].

RYLE -- Ryle, Herbert E. and Elbert Stephens Ryle. *Sone of the Descendants of John Ryle of Anson County, North Carolina and the Ryle Family of Boone County, Kentucky.* Stevensville, MD, 1961. 107 l. [L14885].

RYLE -- Ryle, Herbert E. *The Stephens / Ryle Book: the History and Descendants of Benjamin Stephens, Sr., of Orange County, Virginia and Campbell County, Ky.and John Ryle, Sr., of Anson County, North Carolina Who Died in 1777 and Whose Children Settled in Boone County, Kentucky.* Upper Marlboro, MD, H. E. Ryle, 1987. 454p. 1. Stevens family. 2. Ryle family. 3. Ryle, John, ca.1735-1777-Family. 4. Stephens, Benjamin, 1754-1839-Family. [G578].

RYLE -- Williamson, Mamie. *History of the Ryle Family.* Florence, KY, Fitzgerald, Fitzgerald, 1955. 69, 22 l. [L14884; D10888].

S

SADOWSKI -- Sandusky, A. Clay. *...Polish Pioneers of Virginia and Kentucky, by Miecislaus Haiman, with Notes on Genealogy of the Sadowski Family.* Chicago, IL, Polish R. C. Union of America. 1937. 84p. See also SADOWSKY [G578] immediately below. [L14902; VV].

SADOWSKY -- Haiman, Miecislaus. *Polish Pioneers of Virginia and Kentucky, with Notes on Genealogy of the Sadowsky Family by A. Clay Sandusky.* Chicago, IL, Polish R. C. Union of America, 1937. San Francisco, CA, R and E

Research Associates, 1971. 84p. 1. Polish Americans-Virginia. 2. Polish Americans-Kentucky. 3. Sadowsky family. [G578].

SAGESER -- Knour, Osee Johnson and John Russell Segeser, Jr. *Sageser Genealogy: Descendants of Jacob Segeser, Who Will Was Probated on August 6, 1821 in Fayette County, KY.* Decorah, IA, Anundsen Pub. Co., 1978. 270p. [C607].

SALISBURY -- Parrish, Verle H. *Elder Bill Salisbury Family Records.* Stamping Ground, KY, Parrish, 1980. 81p., 3 leaves of plates. 1. Salisbury family. 2. Floyd County (Ky.)-Genealogy. [G580; C608].

SALISBURY -- Saulsberry, Henry M. *Brochure of Salisbury-Saulsberry Family.* Paintsville, KY, Author, n.d. 21p. 6 leaves. [X-FW].

SAMPLE -- Sample, Trixie Dixon. *Samples, From Pennsylvania to Texas.* Owensboro, KY, Cook-McDowell Publications, 1981. 96, 5, 35p. Family history compiled by Evalyn Parrot Scott. [C609].

SAMUEL -- Hoffman, Muriel M. *Samuel Family Story: Virginia, Kentucky, Indiana, Illinois.* Anchor, IL, 1971. [VV].

SANDERS -- Harris, Mrs. Merie Hicks. *The Sanders Family of Virginia, Kentucky, Ohio & Iowa.* Cedar Rapids, IA, 1977. 28 l. [NG87].

SANDERS -- Sanders, Walter R. *Robert Sanders and John Sanders of Adair County, Kentucky.* Lichtfield, IL, 1949. 13p. [X-FW].

SANDIFER -- Ruggles, Carrola Sandeful and Arthur Lee McLaughlin. *The Sandefur Family History.* Owensboro, KY, McDowell Publs., 1981. 120 leaves. [C610].

SAUNDERS -- Downs, Barry W. *The Sanders Family of Edmonson County, Kentucky: First*

Family of the Forks. Leichtfield, KY B. W. Downs, 1989. viii, 209p., 1 leaf of plates. 1. Saunders family. 2. Kentucky-Genealogy. [G583].

SAUNDERS -- Sanders, Carol Lee. *Sanders, Dickerson, Burchett and Related Families.* Pellyton, KY, C. L. Sanders, 1984. 130p. [C612].

SAUNDERS -- Sanders, Walter Ray. *The Sanders of Kentucky, A Family History.* Lichtfield, IL, 1946. 1, 22 numb. l. [L15027].

SAVAGE -- Savage, Jacob Cochran. *We Are The Savages: Descendants of Ensign Thomas Savage of Jamestown.* Wurtland, KY, Savage, 1974. xiv, 64p. [S2171; D10985].

SAYLOR -- Fee, Holly. *Saylor Family Footprints: Being the Family and Descendants of Solomon & Sarah Saylor of Harlan County, Kentucky.* Harlan, KY, Footprints Publications & Research. 1987. 53, 12p. 1. Saylor family. 2. Saylor, Solomon, ca.1760-1848-Family. 3. Kentucky-Genealogy. [G585].

SCALF -- Scalf, Henry P. *Chronicles of the Scalf Family.* Stanville, KY, 1970. 206p. [A589].

SCOTT -- Cronbaugh, Lois W. *Descendants of Joseph and Mary Cain Scott of Virginia and Kentucky.* NP, 1976. xli, 222 leaves. [D11086].

SCOTT -- Cronbaugh, Lois E. W. *Descendants of Joseph and Mary Cain Scott of Virginia and Kentucky.* Cedar Rapids, IA, 1976. [VV].

SCOTT -- DeVerter, Ruth H. *John Scott, Sr. Family of Bourbon County, Ky., and Wayne County, Ind.* Baytown, TX, n.d. p. 106-163. [X-FW].

SCOTT -- DeVerter, Ruth (Hendricks). *The Genealogy of the Scott and Galloway Families;*

Scotland, Mifflin County, Pennsylvania, (and) Bourbon County, Kentucky. Baytown, TX, 1959, xiii, 379 l. [L15188].

SEARCY -- Mason, Ruth Fothergill. *The Searcy Family.* Union Kentucky, Mason, 1975. 47, ix leaves. [D11133].

SEARS -- Smith, W. Wayne. *Sears Family of Rowan County, North Carolina, Nicholas County, Kentucky, Indiana, and Missouri.* Moscow, ID, Author, n.d. 18p. [X-FW].

SEAY -- Sanders, Faye Sea. *Leonard Seay: Descendants and Kinfolk.* Louisville, KY, F. S. Sanders, 1984. 115p. 1. Seay family. 2. Seay, Leonard, 1774-1842-Family. 3. Kentucky-Genealogy. [G595; DC3250].

SEDGWICK -- Knox, Joan Ritchie. [G595]. See above: CANBY. [G118].

SEWARDS -- *Benjamin Franklin Sewards Senior of Dry Ridge, Kentucky and Clark County, Indiana.* NP, 1966. 32, 38 leaves. [D11191].

SHACKLEFORD -- Kaiser, Mary J. *First Collection of Some Statistics and Known Facts on Descendants of Richard Shackelford and Wife, Elizabeth Dean, of Mercer Co., Ky. (ca. 1810-1974).* Fort Wayne, IN, 1974. 89p. [X-FW].

SHANNON -- Stimpson, Roberta Shannon. *Shannon Family Research Kentucky, Tennessee, Virginia and Other States.* Berkley, VA, Stimpson, 1987. 253p. [DC3275].

SHARP -- Montgomery, Anne Deubery. *Sharps of Augusta County, Virginia, Redford County Virginia and Three Soldiers of the Revolution Came to Kentucky. Rev 1971.* San Francisco, CA, 1971. 56p. [S2244; VV].

SHARP -- Smutz, Harold Turk. *George Sharp (Sharpe) of Virginia and Kentucky and Some of*

His Descendants in Knox County, Missouri. NP, 1970. 11 leaves. [A600].

SHELBURNE -- Stevenson, Kenyon. *Shelburnes of Old Virginia: From the Arrival of Thomas, The Emigrant, in 1607 to the Time When the Children of Augustine Came From Kentucky to Indiana.* Akron, OH, n.d. [VV].

SHELBY -- Wilson, Samuel M. *Susan Hart Shelby, a Memoir (with Genealogy).* Lexington, KY, 1923. 66p. [X-LI].

SHELTON -- Shelton, Kenneth A. *The Shelton Trek Across Kentucky: The History of the Jeremiah Shelton Family in Kentucky and Missouri.* Farminton, MO, K. A. Shelton, 1987. 72, 12p. 1. Shelton family. 2. Shelton, Jeremiah, ca. 1745-1829-Family. 3. Kentucky-Genealogy. 4. Missouri-Genealogy. [G604].

SHIPP -- Sanders, Walter Ray. *The Shipp Genealogy from Essex County, Virginia, to Kentucky and Indiana.* Litchfield, IL. 1946. 50 leaves. [NG89].

SHIPP -- Sanders, Walter Ray. *The Shipp Genealogy.* NP, 1956. 141 l. [D11329].

SHORT -- Baer, Mabel Van Dyke. *Short Families of Kentucky and Virginia.* NP, 1966. 173 l. [D11361; VV].

SIMMONS -- Harris, Milton Stephen. *Black Family Tree: "Slavery to 1984".* Owensboro, KY, M. S. Harris, 1984. 60p. [C638].

SIMS -- Prewitt, Lela Wolfe. *Ancestors & Descendants of Thomas Sims of Culpeper County, Virginia, Edmund Butler of Virginia and Kentucky with Allied Families & Other Culpeper Data.* Fairfield, IA, 1972. vi, 194p. [S2299; VV].

SIMS -- Shoemaker, Mary Ann Dickerson. *James Alfred Sims, A Kentucky Descendant of the Maryland Semmes.* Oakton, VA, Shoemaker, 1990. 114p. [DC3349].

SINKHORN -- McGee, Teresa Sinkhorn. *The Sinkhorn Family History -- 1st ed.* -- Danielsville, KY, T. S. McGee, 1983. ca 250p in various pagings. [C639].

SIPE -- Brock, Freda Marie Guymon. *Ancestors and Descendants of Henry Sipes, Breckenridge County, Kentucky, 1655-1985.* Fairfield, IL, F. M. Brock, 1985. 228p. 1. Sipe family. 2. Sipe, Henry, ca.1763-ca.1827-Family. [G612].

SISCO -- Nacke, Judy. [G612]. See above: COX. [G162].

SISK -- Sisk, Luther L. *The Sisk Family: Virginia--North Carolina--South Carolina--Kentucky--Alabama--Tennessee--Georgia--Missouri--Texas.* Escondido, CA,1980. 1 v. various foliations. [C640; VV].

SKETOE -- Young, Laurie. [G613]. See above: DONAHUE. [G195].

SLOAN -- Slone, Verna Mae. *What My Heart Wants to Tell.* Washington, DC, New Republic Books, 1979. xiii, 143p., 4 l. of plates. 1. Slone, Verna Mae, 1914- 2. Knott County, (Ky.)-Biography. 3. Sloan family. 4. Knott County (Ky.)-Social life and customs. [G614].

SLOAN -- Tully, Eleanor Laura Slone. *The Creekway -- A Family Anthology.* Pippa Passes, KY, Pippa Valley Print, 1983. 106p. [C644].

SMITH -- Hall, William K. *Smith Family of Fleming County, Kentucky, Peoria County, Illinois (and) Linn County, Oregon: Being Descendants of Robert Smith, Who Died in 1798 in Fleming County, Kentucky.* Springfield, MO, n.d. 14 leaves. [X-OS].

SMITH -- Hawkins, Mildred Smith Curd. *The Family of Joseph H. and Sally (Covington) Smith of Warren County, Kentucky, 1808-1971.* Bowling Green, KY, 1971. x, 103p. [S2324; NG91].

SMITH -- Hieronymous, Goldie Smith (Mrs. George Hieronymous. *Descendants of Nathaniel Smith, Knox/Whitley County, Kentucky, Son of Elijah Smith -- Revolutionary War Patrior from New Jersey and Virginia.* Arlington, VA, Falls Church, VA, 1982. 220p. [C646; DS667].

SMITH -- Jillson, Willard Rouse. *A Bibliography of the Life and Writings of Col. James Smith.* Frankfort, KY, Kentucky Historical Society, 1947. 51p. [D11546].

SMITH -- Smith, Ballard, Jr. *A Genealogical Record of the Smiths of Oyster River from the First Settler in 1630 to 1874; with Some Account of the Immediate Ancestors of the Honorable Valentine Smith and His Descendents (sic).* Louisville, KY, Courier-Journal Print., 1875. 28p. [L15792].

SMITH -- Smith, Pearl O. *Peter Smith: Some of His Virgina, North Carolina, and Kentucky Descendants.* Washington, DC, 1976. 71, 13, 13 leaves, 12 leaves of plates. [C648; VV].

SNEAD -- Srokes(sic) , William E., Jr. *An American Saga; The Story of the Snead Family of Accomac County, Virginia, and of Kentucky.* North Garden, (VA), 1952. [VV].

SNODGRASS -- Anderson, Lola. *Snodgrass of Butler County, Kentucky.* Tucson, AZ, L. Anderson, 1982. A-I, 349 leaves. [C650].

SNYDER -- Horlacher, Vaneta Thomas & Levi Jackson Horlacher. *Family of John and Anna Margaret Lowald Snyder of Northampton and Centre Counties, Pennsylvania. 1st ed.* Lexington, KY, V. T. & L. J. Horlacher, 1972. 175p. [S2343; NG91; D11656; VP].

SNYDER -- Lawson, Ernest M. *Snyder Family; The Descendants of William C. and Lydia (Dickey) Snyder.* Burkesville, KY, 1978. 100p. [NG91].

SNYDER -- Snyder, Joseph B. *History of the Family of Snyder, Schneider, Snider, More*

Particularly of the Branch Headed by Frederick and Son William of Whitley County, Kentucky. Harlan, KY, (St. Louis) 1st St. Louis Law Printing Co., Snyder, 1940. iv, 72p. DC gives 72, viii p. [L15948; DC3403].

SOLOMON -- Clay, Grady. [G621]. See above: ROBERTS. [G560].

SOLOMON -- Stiles, Jessie Vernon and Lillie Edith (Sharum) Smith. *The Family of Wilson Salmon: Wilson Salmon, Native of Kentucky, Immigrant to Indiana and Missouri, and His Descendants Which Includes (sic) the Sharum, Morland, & Kindell Branches.* Salt Lake City, UT, E. Smith, 1982. Alan's Print Shop. 122p. [C653].

SOUDER -- Marx, Hazel R. Dick. *The Descendants of George Harley Souter and Jane Petherham Souter.* Utica, KY, McDowell Publications, 1988. 195p. 1. Souder family. 2. Souter, George Harley, 1839-1912-Family. 3. Michigan-Genealogy. [G623].

SOUTH -- Gee, Christine South. *Genealogical Notes on the South Family from New Jersey, Pennsylvania, Maryland, Virginia, South Carolina, Kentucky, and Texas.* Greenville, SC, 1963. v, 163p. [L15974; VV].

SOWERS -- Bowling, Noland. *Meet Your Ancestors: Siers, Sowers, Sours, and Allied Families, 1740-1980.* Owensboro, KY, McDowell Publications, 1981. 548, xlix p., 17 pages of plates. [C655].

SPALDING -- Spalding, John Lancaster. *A Kentucky Pioneer.* NP, 1932. xix, 111p. [D11694].

SPARKS -- NAS. *The Sparks Quarterly: The Official Publication of the Sparks Family Association.* Louisville, KY, The Association, 1953-. _ v. Indexes for vols 21-30 bound separately. See DAR Shelflist for Library Holdings. [DC3414].

SPAULDING -- Spalding, Hughes. *The Spalding Family of Maryland, Kentucky and Georgia. A History of How the Pioneer Catholic Spalding Family in America Originated in Maryland and Spread to Kentucky, Georgia and Other States.* Atlanta, GA, 1963-65. 2 v. - V. 1. 1658 to 1963; - V. 2. 1658 to 1965. [L16014].

SPEED -- Heywood, John H. *Judge John Speed and His Family.* Louisville, KY, John P. Morton & Co., 1894. 35p. D gives 35 l. [L16024; D11710].

SPEED -- Speed, Thomas. *Records and Memorials of the Speed Family.* Louisville, KY, Courier Journal Job Printing Co., 1892. 206p. [L16023; D11711].

SPELLMAN -- Carter, Lennie M. *The Spillman Family of Lawrence Co., Ky.* Timonium, MD, L. M. Carter, 1987. iii, 135p. Additions and corrections entitled: Spillman spillovers (12 leaves) published separately, 1988, in pocket. 1. Spellman family. 2. Lawrence County (Ky.)-Genealogy. [G625].

SPENCER -- Hardin, Bayless. *Revolutionary Ancestors of Julia Spencer (Mrs. William Breckenridge) "Roccliegan", Paris, Bourbon County, Kentucky.* Frankfort, KY, 193_. Genealogical Table. [L16035].

SPOON -- Spohn, Onna Jean. *The Spohn Story.* Utica, KY, McDowell Publications, 1987. 662p. 1. Spoon family. 2. Spohn, Jennifer Louise, 1966- . [G627].

SPOONAMORE -- Smutz, Harold Turk. *Philip Spoonamore, Sr. and Jr., of Kentucky and Some of Their Descendants in Illinois, Indiana, Missouri, and Texas.* NP, 1970. 12 l. [S2362].

SPOTSWOOD -- Fontaine, Wm. Winston, A. M. *The Descent of General Robert E. Lee, From King Robert the Bruce, of Scotland.* A paper before the Southern Historical Association, of

Louisville, KY., March 29, 1881. NP, 1881. 6p., 1 leaf. [L16060; VV].

STAMM -- Ronsheim, Edw. J. Sr. *The Stamm Family of Ohio and Kentucky*. Anderson, IN, 1954. 24 l. [L16118].

STANDARD -- Standard, Charles Martin. *The Standard, Higgins, and Related Families: Genealogical History of Two Pioneer Kentucky Families and Their Related Families*. Dallas, TX, Standard, 1979. vi, 459p. [C660].

STANDIFORD -- NAS. *Standiford Family: I. In Maryland, 1687-1784... II. In Kentucky, 1784-1933... III. In Indiana, 1817-1933... Descendants of William Standiford Who Lived in Hopewell, Md., 1687*. NP, 1935. 16 leaves, folded chart, bound with supplement and index... 9 leaves. [X-FW].

STANFIELD -- Hieronymous, Goldie Smith. *Descendants of Sampson Stanfield, Who Went from Anson County, North Carolina into Knox County, Kentucky, in the Early 1800's, was So n of John Stanfield and Wife Mary*. Falls Church, VA, Hieronymous, 1978, 158p. Rev. ed. published as Descendants of Sampson Stanfield, who went from Anson County, North Carolina into Knox County, Kentucky in the early 1800's. Rev. ed. 1981. [C661].

STANTON -- Mahoney, William James, Jr. *The Stantons of Kentucky*. NP, Mahoney, 1977. vii, 256p. [C662].

STARK -- Abbott, Jane H. *Jeremiah Stark of Culpeper County, Va., Later of Allen County, Ky. and Some Descendants. Genealogical Notes and Records*. NP, 1930. 64 l. [L16181; VV].

STARK -- *Stark Family of N.H., Va., Ky., and Conn*. NP, n.d. 11p. 10 leaves. [X-FW; VV].

STARKS -- Starks, John P. *Genealogy of the Starks, Price, Berry, and Crutcher Families*. Louisville, KY, 1920. 72p. [X-CH/FW/LI].

STARRETT -- Starrett, Elizabeth Regenstein. *Starrett and Allied Families Including the Virginia and Kentucky Ancestry of Elizabeth Regenstein Starrett and Over 40 Other Early American Connections.* Berryville, VA, The Prince Maccus Publishers, 1981. viii, 237p. [DS686].

STEEL -- Fitzgerald, Anne LeGrande. *Miscellaneous Data on Steel-Steele Family of Kentucky.* NP, 1950. 43 l. [D11868].

STEPHENS -- Calvert, John. *John Calvert's Notebook; Containing Data on the Stephens and Ryle Families... of Boone County, Ky.* Florence, KY, Fitzgerald, 1956. 27, 7 leaves. [X-FW].

STEPHENS -- Scalf, Henry P. *Stephens Family.* Dayton, OH, C. E. Shepard, 1970. 68p. Reprint of Data Gathered by Henry Scalf and pub. in 1956 in the Floyd Co., (Ky.) Times. With a chart of C. E. Shepard. [X-FW].

STEPP -- Scalf, Henry Preston and Randolph W. Stepp. *The Stepp/Stapp Families of America: A Source Book. -- Rev. ed.* Stanville, KY, Scalf, 1976. 421p. S gives date of 1974. [C665; S2388; NG93].

STEPP -- Scalf, Henry Preston. *The Stepp/ Stapp Families of America.* NP, nd, 426p. [D11914].

STERN -- Stearns, Monyene. *The Stearns Family Scrapbook.* McGregor, TX, Stearns Enterprises 1985. 135p. 1. Stearn family. 2. Kentucky-Genealogy. 3. Texas-Genealogy. [G633].

STERNER -- Sterner, Pauline L. *The Ancestry of the Families in Hancock County, Ohio of Alge, Beck, Schaller, Sterner, and Weitz, and Batcheldor, Clarke, and Lilly in Nelson County, Kentucky.* Findlay, OH, Sterner, 1976. x, 51p. [C666].

STERRETT -- Starrett, Elizabeth Regenstein. *Starrett and Allied Families: Including the Virginia and Kentucky Ancestry of Elizabeth Regenstein Starrett and Over 40 Other Early American Connections.* Berryville, VA, Prince Maccus Publishers, 1981. xiii, 237p. [C666].

STEVENS -- Ryle, Herbert E. [G634]. See above: RYLE. [G578].

STEVENS -- Stevens, Albert C. *Stevens Family Record.* Louisville, KY, 1959. 439 leaves. Includes newspaper clippings from the author and "Stevens - Mathes reunion" 1959. [X-NY].

STEVENS -- Stevens, Albert C. *Record of the Family of John Stevens, Staten Island, N. Y., Orange Co., Va., and Shelby Co., Ky.* Louisville, KY, 1961. 1 vol. loose-leaf. [X-NY; VV].

STEVENS -- Jones, Winona. *Our Royal Ancestors.* Lexington, KY, Transylvania Printing Co., 1971. 143p. [S2394; D11927].

STEVENSON -- Stevenson, Margaret. *Stevenson Family History; From the Eastern Shore of Maryland (Old Somerset renamed Worcester County) to Woodford, Kentucky, to Putnam County, Indiana, with Allied Families.* New York, NY, 1966. 162p. [L16310].

STEWART -- Stone, Martha Jane. *The Genealogy and History of the Stewart Family of Halifax County, Virginia, Caswell and Person Counties, North Carolina, Trigg County, Kentucky.* Lexington, KY, 1986. 141p. [NG94].

STILES -- Pence, LaFayette Stiles. *A History of the Kentucky and Missouri Stiles.* Lebanon, KY, W. T. Hawkins, 1896. 45p. [L16329; D11973].

STILES -- Sparks, Lois Ogden Stiles. *A History of the David Stiles Family: A*

Genealogy 1575-1980: An Inclusion of the Works of Four Previous Historians. Murray, KY, Creative Printers, 1980. x, 479p. [C668].

STILES -- Stiles, Lewis Ogden. *The Family of David Stiles, of the Ten Tribes of the House of David. The Ancestry and Posterity of David Stiles, an Immigrant to Kentucky.* Louisville, KY, Mayes Printing Co., 1939. 310p. [L16333; D11977].

STIMSON -- Crain, Luther N. [G635]. See above: CRANE. [G163; C157].

STINNETT -- Stinnett, Charles Dunn. *Stinnett, Dunn, Atkins, and Glen: A 200 Year History, 1777-1977.* Lexington, KY, C. D. Stinnett, 1977. 108p., 16 pages of plates. Folded Genealogical Table laid in. [C668].

STINSON -- Crain, Luther N. [G635]. See above: CRANE. [G163].

STONE -- Armstrong, Virginia Stone. *Our Stone Family from England to Kentucky.* Utica, KY, McDowell Publications, 1990. 258p. 1. Stone family. 2. England-Genealogy. 3. Kentucky-Genealogy. [G637].

STOUT -- Baganz, Herbert M. *The Decedent (sic) of Richard, 1615-1705, & Penolpe (sic) Stout, 1622-1732, & Generations Thru to Belle S. (Clift) Baganz: Also Exerpts from Kentucky History, 1801-1850: Events, Individuals, Religions, Which Pertained to Those Persons Living There During This Period.* Lafayette, IN, H. M Baganz, 1972. 86 leaves. 1. Stout family. 2. Stout, Richard, ca.1611-1705-Family. 3. Baganz, Belle S. Clift, b.1898-Family. Kentucky-Genealogy. [G638].

STOUT -- Lillard, Jacques Ephraim Stout. *The Stout Family of New York City and the State of Kentucky.* Washington, DC, 1939. 2p., 2 Genealogical Tables. NG does not show pages. [L16438; NG94].

STOUT -- Lillard, Ephraim Stout. *The Stout, Disney, Clinton, Morrison, Grey of Ruthyn Magna Carta & Royal Descent.* Washington, DC, Court of Neptune Press, 1945. Genealogical Table. [L16442].

STROUD -- Headrick, Marcella Pickerel. [G641]. See above: HAGAN. [G288].

STUART -- Denham, Marion Lee. [G642]. See above: FOSTER. [G236].

STUART -- Evett, Leila F. *Descendants of Josh Stewart & Polly Stutzman.* Utica, KY, McDowell Publications, 1986. iv, 632p. 1. Stuart family. 2. Stewart, Josh, 1929/30-1925-Family. 3. Oklahoma-Genealogy. [G642].

STUART -- Fox, Martha Stuart. [G642]. See above: QUISENBERRY. [G539].

STUART -- Sanders, Robert Stuart. *The Reverend Robert Stuart, D.D., 1772-1856 a Pioneer in Kentucky Presbyterianism and His Descendants.* Louisville, KY, The Dunne Press, 1962. 167p. [D12110; X-FW/NY].

STUART -- Stone, Martha Jane. *The Genealogy and History of the Stewart Family of Halifax County, Virginia, Caswell and Person Counties North Carolina, Trigg County, Kentucky.* Lexington, KY, M. J. Stone, 1986-<1987 >. v. <1-2 >. [G643].

STURGEON -- Wood, Edith. *A Genealogical History of the Sturgeon, Elder, and Allied Families of Kentucky.* Louisville, KY, 1968. 97 leaves. [X-FW/NY].

SULLIVAN -- Sanders, Walter R. *Sullivan Families of Taylor County, Kentucky.* Lichtfield, IL, n.d. 16p. [X-FW].

SUMMERS -- Hammers, Marian G. *John and Richard Sumner and Their Descendants.* Utica, KY, McDowell Publications, 1986. 154p. 1. Summers family. 2. Sumner, John, ca.1765-

ca.1837-Family. 3. North Carolina-Genealogy. [G645].

SURBER -- Vance, Vida Surber. *The Missouri & Kentucky Surbers and Their Descendants: A Study of the Ancestry and Posterity of Henry Surber: A Virginia Colonist of the Eighteen(th) Century, from ca. 1700-1978.* Mexico, MO, 1985. [VV].

SUTHERLAND -- Hudson, Florence Sutherland. *"We Cousins" (Virginia to Texas). A Genealogy of Several of the Families Comprising the Alabama Settlement of Austin's County, 1830 and 1831, now Texas, and Including the Other Virginia Lines of the Sutherland Family.* San Benito, TX, 1957 - v. [L16634; VV].

SUTHERLAND -- Sutherland, Henry C. *Sutherland Records Found in Georgia, Illinois, Indiana, Kentucky, Maryland, North Carolina, South Carolina and Virginia.* Crown Point, IN, 1968. 245p. [L16635].

SUTTON -- De Marce, Virginia Easley. *The Sutton Families of Boone and Pike Cos., Mo., Bourbon, Co., Ky., and Culpeper County, Va.* Arlington, VA, De Marce, 1988. 146 l. A Genealogy of the Interrelated Easley, Fortney, Sutton, Cheavens, Self, and Black Families of Boone County, Mo; Chapter 3. [DC3555].

SUTTON -- Goldsborough, C. R. T. *William Loftus Sutton, M.D., 1797-1862: Father of the Ky. State Medical Soc...* Lexington, KY, 1948. 246p. [X-FW].

SUTTON -- Goldsborough, Carrie Tarleton and Anna Goldsborough Fisher. *Descendants of John Sutton and His Wife, Temperance Lane.* Lexington, KY, Clay Printing Co.,1941. ix, 179p. [L16645; D12174].

SWARTZWELDER -- McCann, William R. *Ancestors - Descendants of John I. Jones Who Married Mary Ellen Swartzwelder (a McCann)... Family of Samuel Swartzwelder...* NP, 1956. 19p. [XA-SW].

SWEET -- Calhoun, Logan E. [G647]. See above: CALHOUN. [G115].

T

TAFFELMEYERS -- Colella, Margaret Bone. *Taffelmeyers / Tofflemires Here and There with Associated Families.* Hartford, KY, Owensboro, KY, McDowell Publications, 1979. iv, 407p. [C681; NG95].

TANDY -- Sanders, Walter R. *Smyth Tandy, 1741-1823, Virginia Gentleman and Kentucky Pioneer.* Litchfield, IL, Sanders, 1948. 41 leaves. [D12246; X-FW/MH/NY/SP; VV].

TANNER -- Hussey, Marguerite Carleton. *The Family of Rev. John Tanner - Baptist Preacher; Virginia - North Carolina - Kentucky - Missouri.* Berkeley, CA, 1972. [VV].

TANNER -- Lloyd, Emma Rouse. *Tanner Family of Virginia and Kentucky.* NP, n.d. Pages not shown. (Available for Consultation at the Lloyd Library, 309 West Court St., Cincinnati, OH.) [L16768].

TARLETON -- Goldsborough, Carrie Tarleton and Anna Goldsborough Fisher. *Tarleton Records Containing the Descendants of the Three Brothers, John, Jeremiah, and Caleb Turleton of Maryland and Kentucky and Caleb Tarleton of West Virginia.* Atlanta, GA, Williams Print Co., 1950. 214p. [L16781].

TARVIN -- Torrey, Alice Ellenor Herndon. *Tarvin Family Connectors and Cracroft Families of Mason County and Campbell Co., Ky.* Wilder, KY, R. Brennan, 1977. 25, 24 leaves. [C683].

TAYLOR -- NAS. *Taylor Family Association, Incorporated. Year Books... v. 1-2, 1924-29.* Louisville, KY, 1926- 2 v. [L16818].

TAYLOR -- NAS. *Yearbook of the Taylor Family Assoc. 1924-1926.* Louisville, KY, 1926. v. 1. 35p. [X-LI].

TAYLOR -- Brewer, Mary Taylor. *From Log Cabins to the White House: A History of the Taylor Family.* Wooten, KY, M. T. Brewer, 1985. ix, 5, 522p. 1. Taylor family. 2. Taylor, Zachary, 1784-1850-Family. 3. Virginia-Genealogy. [G652; C684].

TAYLOR -- O'Gorman, Ella F. *Taylor Family of Harrison County, Kentucky.* Los Angeles, CA, 1944. 15 leaves. [X-LA].

TAYLOR -- Stinson, Era W. *Williams, Walker, Taylor, and Allied Families.* Bowling Green, KY, E. E. Stinsson, 1986. i, 68 leaves. 1. Williams family. 2. Walker family. 3. Taylor family. [G652].

TAYLOR -- Taylor, L. Rhea. *Pioneers Moses Taylor and Elizabeth Prevatte Taylor, sr. of Kentucky and North Carolina. 1968 Revision.* Bowling Green, KY, L. R. Taylor, 1968. 145 leaves. [X-FW/NY].

TAYLOR -- Taylor, Reubemia. *The Taylor Family in Virginia and Kentucky, 1650-1900.* NP, 1953. 29 l. [D12311; VV].

TAYLOR -- Taylor, Walter Kingsley. *The Lives, Families and Descendants of Arnold, Phillip, and Benjamin Taylor: from Pennsylvania and New Jersey to Kentucky.* Winter Park, FL, W. K. Taylor, 1984. viii. 225p. C and VP list under ARNOLD (?). [G653; C20: VP].

TEAGUE -- Cunningham, Agnes T. *History and Genealogy of the Teague Pioneers of Christina County, Ky.* NP, 1971. 249p. [X-PH].

TEAGUE -- Cunningham, Agnes Teague and Wetona Franklin Harrell. *Teague; Tighe; Tigue; MacTaighg; Taighg; O'Taighg.* Nortonville, KY, 1971. 249p. [S2464; X-FW].

TEATER -- Teater, Howard Glen, Patsy Teator Benton & Howard, Curry Teator. *The Kentucky Teator Family.* Helena, AL, The Authors, 1974.

297p. D shows 296p. and no place of publication. G lists under TEETERS. 1. Teeters family. [G654; S2472; DC3601].

TERRY -- Bushnell, Edna Harris. *Terry Records of Virginia.* Owensboro, KY, McDowell Publs, 1980. 2, 243p. [C687; D12344; VV].

TERRY -- Ingmire, Frances T. *Terry and Allied Families of Virginia, Kentucky, Illinois, Texas.* Creve Coeur, MO, Ingmire, 1976. 2 vols. [C687; X-FW/NY; VV].

THOMAS -- Bridges, Gilbert N. *History and Genealogy of James & Molly (Stanley) Thomas and Drewry & Charity (Calhoon) Bridges.* Uniontown, KY, Bridges, 1964. 438p. [D12367].

THOMAS -- Bridges, Troy H. *Thomas and Bridges Family History.* Louisville, KY, Bridges, 1960. 51 l. [D12368].

THOMAS -- Dodele, Mabel Maxine. *A Trace of Thomas.* Utica, KY, McDowell Publications, 1984. 305p. [C688].

THOMAS -- Horlacher, Vaneta Thomas and Levi Jackson Horlacher. *Thomas -- Huffines Family of Hancock County, Kentucky, Indiana. -- 1st ed. --* Lexington, KY, Horlacher, 1980. ca. 200 leaves in various foliations. [C689].

THOMAS -- Thomas, Edison H. *The Thomas and Bridges Story, 1540-1840.* Louisville, KY, T & E Publishers, 1972. 180p. S indicates 1st ed. [S2478; D12382].

THOMPSON -- Agricola, David V. *Descendants of John Thompson, 1783-1854, of Lawrence County, Kentucky.* Lakewood, OH, Agricola, 1976. iii, 19p. [C690; X-FW].

THOMPSON -- Thompson, Frances Gertrude. *Genealogy of One Robert Thompson Family: Maryland Colonist, Kentucky Pioneers, U.S.A.* Catherine, KY, Thompson, 1976. 46, 7 l. [DC3640].

TIMMONS -- Corum, Frank. *Captain George Timmons, Fact and Fiction.* Hanson, KY, Corum, 1990. 1 v. in various pagings. [DC3652].

THRELKELD -- Threlkeld, Hansford Lee. *Threlkeld Genealogy.* Morganfield, KY, Threlkeld, 1932. 336p. [L17043; D12456].

THRELKELD -- Threlkeld, Hansford Lee. *Threlkeld Genealogy.* Evansville, IN, Unigraphic, 1979. 336p., 8 l. Reprint. Originally published: Morganfield, KY, H. L. Threlkeld, 1932. [G661].

THRELKELD -- Williamson, Mamie. *Threlkeld Family Data, Copied by William and Anne Fitzgerald.* Florence, KY, 1954. 3 leaves. [L17044].

THROCKMORTON -- Throckmorton, Charles Wickliffe. *The Descendants of the Honorable Thomas Throckmorton, Born 1739 in Virginia, and Died at "Rich Hill", Kentucky, 1826.* New York, NY, 1898. Genealogical Table. [L17046].

THRUSTON -- Jennings, Kathleen. *Louisville's First Families; A Series of Genealogical Sketches, with Drawings by Eugenia Johnson.* Louisville, KY, The Standard Printing Co., 1920. 176p. Contains the Bullitt, Prather, Clark, Churchill, Pope, Speed, Joyes, Veech, Thompson, Taylor, Bate, and Floyd Families. [L17058a].

TIPPIN -- Tippin, James Jackson. *Ancestry of Sanford Lathadeus Tippin Family of Henderson County, Kentucky.* Shreveport, LA, M. L. Bath Co., 1940. 38p. [D12517].

TIPTON -- Heinemann, Charles Brunk. *Tipton Family of Maryland, Virginia, Tennessee, Kentucky, Ohio, Indiana, Illinois, Missouri.* Washington, DC, 1934. 1, 29, 1, 2, 10 numb. leaves. [L17127; VV].

TIPTON -- Heinemann, Charles Brunk. *Tipton Family of Maryland, Virginia, Tennessee,*

Kentucky, Ohio, Indiana, Illinois, Missouri. Chicago, IL, 1937. 1, 40, 11 numb. leaves. [L17128].

TIPTON -- Heinemann, Charles Brunk. *Tipton Family of Maryland, Virginia, Tennessee, Kentucky, Ohio, Indiana, Illinois, Missouri.* Washington, DC, 1941. 1, 48 numb. l. [L17129].

TIPTON -- Heinemann, Charles Brunk. *Tipton Family Records in the Present Boundaries of the United States from Colonial Times to 1950.* Washington, DC, 1950. 332, 49 l. [L17131].

TIPTON -- Tipton, W. Hord. *The Tipton Family History.* Mt. Sterling, KY, Tipton, 1948. 605p. [D12519].

TIPTON -- Tipton, Whitney Hord. The Tipton Family History. Mt. Sterling, KY, Tipton, 1948. 1 v. unpaged. [L17130; D12519].

TOMLINSON -- Tomlinson, George L. *William and Martha Tomlinson of Kentucky, 1749-1844.* Mt. Pleasant, IA, 1932. 14p. [X-FW].

TOMS -- Tomes, Betty Jean Porter. *Thomas Toms / Tomes and His Kentucky Kin.* Utica, KY, McDowell Publications, 1985. 75p. 1. Toms family. 2. Toms, Thomas, ca.1754-1803/4-Family. 3.. Kentucky-Genealogy. [G665; C697].

TOOHEY -- Dromey, John H. *Toohey Family of Knox County, Missouri: Some American Descendants of Patrick and Honora (Ryan) Toohey (living 1830's) of County Clare, Ireland. With Photos by William Gleckler.* Utica, KY, McDowell Publications, 1982. 398p. [C698].

TOWNSEND -- Townsend, Leland Henry, Jr. *Townsend Families in America.* Orange Park, FL, L. H.Townsend, 1985, 1981 (Utica, KY, McDowell Publications). 1 v. (various pagings). 1. Townsend family. [G666].

TRABUE -- Colwell, Pauline Trabue Groves and Knouf, Osee Johnson. *Trabue Family History; Ancestry and Known Descendants of David Trabue, Jr., Born Oct. 9, 1768, Manikintown, Virginia, Died Apr. 8, 1842, Jessamine Co., Kentucky.* Champaign, IL, 1968. 96 leaves. [A665; VV].

TRABUE -- Harper, Lilli DuPuy, Van Culin. *Colonial Men and Times; Containing the Journal of Col. Daniel Traube, Some Account of His Ancestry, Life and Travels in Virginia and the Present State of Kentucky During the Revolutionary Period; The Huguenots, Genealogy, with a Brief Sketch of Allied Families.* Philadelphia, PA, Innes & Sons, 1916. 6, 3-624p. Also Family of DuPuy, p. 367-417. [L17236; VP].

TRAPP -- Trapp, Glenda K. *The Descendants of Johannes & Salome (Schmitt) Trapp (Our Immigrants) 1832-1982.* Utica, KY, McDowell Publications, 1982, 86p. [C701].

TRAVIS -- Travis, Arthur F. *History of the Travis Family in Marshall and Lyon Counties.* Paducah, KY, 1959. 37 leaves. [NG97].

TRAVIS -- Travis, Arthur F. *Meet Grandmother.* Paducah, KY, 1959. 37 leaves. [D12629].

TREADWAY -- Lewis, Ailene Fitch. *The Tredway, Gooch, Embry, Cyphers, and Allied Lines, from England to Maryland, Virginia, Ohio, Kentucky, Illinois: West to North Missouri, Kansas, 1597-1983.* Holden, MO, 1948. 33 l., 2 leaves of plates. [C701; VV].

TROTTER -- Trotter, Susie Eager (Mrs. Isham Patten Trotter, Jr. *Trotter Genealogy. The Virginia - Tennessee - Mississippi Trotter Lines, 1725-1948.* Louisville, KY, Mayes Printing Co., 1948. 225p. [L17332; D12664].

TROUT -- Britt, Daniel S. [G670]. See above: BRITT. [G89; C703].

TRUEBLOOD -- Anderson, Frank E. *Trueblood Family, 1600-1960; Descendants of Caleb Trueblood-Louvina Brooks, 1763-1960.* Louisville, KY, Author, 1960. 44p. [X-FW].

TRUESDALE -- Truesdale, Karl. *Descendants of John Truesdale of Cumberland Co., Pennsylvania.* NP, 1952. 79, 100, 70 leaves. Bound with Trusdells of Kentucky, Descendants of John Truesdel of South Carolina and James Truesdale of Rochester, New York. [DC3698].

TUBBS -- Schermerhorn, Sharon Minor. *The Tubbs and Quinton Families of Pulaski County, Kentucky: Including Family Lines of Anderson, Blackstone, Bolling, Bull, Combs, Dane, (Doyne) de Barette, Farmer, Griffin, Nance, Penley, Stevens, Swearingen, Ware, Weaver, Young, and Zek: Following Lines Added April, 1983: Archdale, Cloud, Harding, Mason.* Olympia, WA, S. M. Schermerhorn, 1983. 219 leaves. [C705].

TUBBS -- Schermerhorn, Sharon Minor. [G672]. See above: ANDERSON. [G13].

TUCKER -- Tucker, Reuel Walter. *Memoirs and History of the Peyton Tucker Family; Ancestors and Descendants of England, Wales, Vermont, Massachusetts, Maryland, Virginia, the Carolinas, Georgia, Tennessee, Kentucky, Illinois, Missouri, Arkansas, Louisiana, Texas, Oklahoma, and California; and Genealogy.* Baltimore, MD, Gateway Press, 1975. xxvii, 256 p. 2 fold. leaves of plates. [S2558; VV].

TULEY -- Tuley, William Floyd. *The Tuley Family Memoirs; an Historical, Biographical and Genealogical Story of the Tuley and Floyd Family Connection in Virginia, Kentucky, and Indiana.* New Albany, IN, W. J. Hedden printer, 1906. v, 6-75p. [L17383].

TURNER -- Lloyd, Emma Rouse. *Turner Family of Virginia and Kentucky.* NP, n.d. Pages not shown. (Available for Consultation at the

Lloyd Library, 309 West Court St., Cincinnati, OH.) [L17408; VV].

U

UNDERWOOD -- Coke, Ben H. *The Underwood Family from Madison County, Virginia.* Utica, KY, McDowell Publications, 1986. viii, 157p. 1. Underwood family. 2. Virginia-Genealogy. [G679].

UNGER -- Unger, Dana and Ada. *The History of the Family of John Henry Ludwig Unger and Gesche Walters Unger.* Ownesboro, KY, McDowell Publications, 1982. 100, xiii p. [C710].

UTT -- Utt, Claire. *Utt-Ventures.* Owensboro, KY, McDowell Publications, 1982. xvi, 539p. [DS720].

V

VANCE -- Dixon, Elizabeth Williamson. *The Vance Family of Virginia, Pennsylvania, North Carolina, Tennessee; the Brank Family of North Carolina and Kentucky.* NP, 1958. 315 l. [D12825; VP; VV].

VANCE -- Garrett, Hester Elizabeth. [G684]. See above: BELCHER. [G46].

VanDEREN -- McMurtry, David Cornelius. *Three VanDeren Sisters of Owen County, Kentucky.* Lexington, KY, Mil- Mac, 1990. xiv, 298p. [DC3753].

VANDEVEER -- Baer, Mabel Van Dyke. *The Vandeveers of North Carolina, Kentucky, and Indiana.* Richmond, VA, Whittet & Shepperson, 1960. xi, 180p. [A680; D12860].

VAN HOOSE -- Parsons, Charles. *The Van Hoose Family.* Ashland, KY, Economy Print., 1964. 74p. [D12881; X-FW/SW].

VAN HOOSE -- Van Hoose, John See. [G682]. See above. BOONE. [G69].

VAN METER -- Van Meter, Banjamin F. *Genealogies and Sketches of Some Old Families.* Louisville, KY, John P. Morton & Co., 1901. v, 182p. [D12897].

VAN NUYS -- Allen, Carrie E. *A Record of the Family of Isaac Van Nuys (or Vannice) of Harrodsburg, Kentucky, Son of Isaac Van Nuys of Millstone, New Jersey.* Chicago, IL, Allen, 1916. 304, 3p. D gives no place of publication. [D12904; X-CH/FW/LI/NY].

VAN TILBURG -- Hale, Carolyn H. *Van Tilburgh: A History of the Southwestern Ohio Family.* Louisa, KY, C. Hale, 1989. vi, 261p. 1. Van Tilburg family. 2. Ohio-Genealogy. [G684].

VAUGHAN -- Leslie, E. Glen. [G687]. See above: FORD. [G235].

VAUGHN -- Coles, James E. [G687]. See above: CROSS. [G167].

VICKERY -- Smart, Clarissa Ruth Barnes. *The Descendants of Mary Broyles Vickery and Francis Marion Vickery of Wayne County, Kentucky.* Charlottesville, VA, 1884. 646p. [NGS11].

VROOMAN -- Paulson, Ross Evans. *Radicalism & Reform; the Vrooman Family and American Social Thought, 1837-1937.* Lexington, KY, University of Kentucky Press, 1968. xxiii, 299p. "Published for the Organization of American Historians." 1. Vrooman family. 2. United States-Social Organization. [G692].

W

WADE -- Wade, Ophelia R. *Wade - Waid - Waide; A Research Book primarily of Census,*

Cemetary, and Courthouse Records for the States of Ala., Ark., Ga., Ind., Ky., Mass., Mo., N.C., Okla., S.C., Tenn., Texas and Va. Bragg City, MO, Author, 1975. 260p. [X-FW/MH].

WAGNER -- Waggener, Lawrence A. *The Waggener Trace: A Genealogy of the Waggener Family of Virginia, Kentucky, Nebraska, Colorado, Oregon, and California, USA. -- 1st ed.* Portland, OR, Genealogical Forum of Portland, 1985. ii, 138p. [G694; C726; VV].

WAITE -- Thomas, Edison H. *A Letter to Our Children.* Louisville, KY, T & E Publishers, 1983. vi, 148p. [C727].

WALDROP -- Waldrop, Melda B. *Ancestors and Descendants of Martha Ann Isabel Hughes Waldrop.* Murray, KY, Waldrop, 1974. 76 l. [D13040].

WALKER -- Bell, Annie W. Burns. *...Daniel Boone's Predecessors in Kentucky, Authentic History.* Frankfurt, KY, 196_. 180p. [X-FW].

WALKER -- Stinson, Era W. [G696]. See above: TAYLOR. [G652].

WALLACE -- Wallace Allen Maxwell. *William and Chaney Wallace and Their Descendants.* Lexington, KY, 1973. vii, 217p. [S2653].

WALLACE -- Whitsett, William H. *Life and Times of Judge Caleb Wallace, Some Time a Justice of the Court of Appeals of the State of Kentucky.* Louisville, KY, J. P. Morton & Company, printers, 1888. 151p. [L17878].

WALLS -- Brumfield, Marci Conrad. *John P. Walls, 1834/N.C.--1898/Ohio.* Maysville, KY, Brumfield, 1990. 28p. [DC3805].

WALTON -- Hyatt, Henry Middleton. *Descendants of John Walton of Baltimore County, Maryland and Harrison County, Kentucky.* New York, NY, Alma Egan Hyatt Foundation, 1950. 73p. [L17929; D13097].

WALTRIP -- Osborne, Allie Wright and Arthur Lee McLaughlin. *The Waltrip Family History.*Utica, KY, McDowell Publications, 1984, 161p. [C731].

WARD -- Hamilton, Anna L. *The Ward Family: The Genealogy of Daniel Jonas Ward, His Ancestors and Descendants.* Utica, KY, McDowell Publs., Whitesville, KY, Hamilton, 1984. 120p. 1. Ward family. 2. Ward, Daniel Jonas, 1805-1894-Family. [G699; DC3816].

WARD -- McGhee, Lucy K. *Ward Family History of Virginia, Showing Their Links with the States of North Carolina, Tennessee and Kentucky Branches of Wards.* Washington, DC, 1957. 29A, 81, A-I l. [X-FW/NY; VV].

WARD -- Ward, Billie Edyth. *Ward: A Genealogical Record of the Wards of Big Sandy.* Baltimore, MD, Gateway Press, Boons Camp, KY, 645p. 1. Ward family. 2. Big Sandy River Region (Ky. and W. Va.)-Genealogy. [G699].

WARDER -- Warder, Walter. *Warder Family in Virginia, Kentucky, and Illinois.* Cairo, IL, 1934. 82p., 8p. index bound in. [X-FW; VV].

WARE -- Ware, Virgil. *[Picture Gallery, 1900-1944]. V. Ware's Picture Gallery, 1900-1944 -- 1st ed.* -- Liberty, KY, E. W. Hall, 1982. 104p. [C732].

WARF -- Neagles, James C. *The Warf Family of Kentucky.* Washington, DC, J. C. Neagles, 1976. 13 leaves, 1 leaf of plates. [C732].

WARREN -- Murrow, Charles H. *John B. Warren (1786-1854) of Bath County, Ky... James Warren Migrated to Indiana from Ky. in 1825, and Daniel Boatwright.* Des Moines, IA, 1974. Unpaged. [X-FW].

WARREN -- Stone, Martha June. *The Warren Family of Trigg County, Kentucky.* Lexington, KY, M. J. Stone, 1990. 411p. 1. Warren family. 2. Kentucky-Genealogy. [G701].

WARREN -- Warren, Robert Penn. *Portrait of a Father.* Lexington, KY, University Press of Kentucky, 1988. 79p. 1. Warren, Robert Penn, 1905- -Biography-Family. 2. Warren, Robert Franklin. 3. Warren family. 4. Fathers and Sons-United States-Biography. 5. Authors, American-20th century-Biography-Family. [G701].

WARREN -- Watkins, Floyd C. *Then & Now: The Personal Past in the Poetry of Robert Penn Warren.* Lexington, KY, University Press of Kentucky, 1982. xii, 184p. [C733].

WATSON -- McMunn, Martha Watson. *Descendants of Washington B. and Katherine Dearstine Watson.* Utica, KY, McDowell Publications, 1986. i, 42p., 10p. of plates. 1. Watson family. 2. Watson, Washinton Boyd, 1833-1900-Family. [G703].

WATSON -- Twain, Mark. [G703]. See above: DARNELL. [G175].

WATTS -- Heinemann, Charles Brunk. *Edward Watts Family of Virginia and Kentucky.* Kansas City, MO, Heinemann, 193_. ca. 150 leaves. [DC3851].

WATTS -- Watts, William C. *The Watts and Courtney Families.* Smithfield, KY, 1891. 6 leaves. [X-NY].

WEAKLEY -- McNamara, Elizabeth W. *Weakley, Scearce, Arnold, Families of Kentucky.* Baltimore, MD, Gateway Press, 1980. 328p. [D13246].

WEAVER -- Palsgrove, Maxine Lyman. *History of Conrad Weaver, His Wife Rebecca Senseman, and Their Descendants.* Hartford, KY, McDowell Publications, 1978. 25p. [D13256].

WEBB -- Martin, Henry G. *Webb.* Richmond, KY, Martin, 1978. 78 leaves. [D13262].

WEBB -- Martin, Henry G. *Webb. -- 2nd ed,* Richmond, KY, Martin, 1983. 79 l. [C738].

WEBSTER -- Fuchs, Marilyn Worster. *Webster Genealogy.* Ft. Mitchell, KY, Fuchs, Wilson, Wolcott, 1976. 193p. [D13271].

WEBSTER -- Webster, JoAnne Meade. *Indian Hollow Road: A 19th Century American Family, Their Letters, Their Story. Limited Ed.* Louisville, KY, 1984. 2 v. (1074p.) [C739].

WECKMAN -- Conway, Jo Ann. *Weisenberger - Weckman Family History.* Utica, KY, McDowell Publications, 1984. 141p. 1. Weissenberger family. 2. Weckman family. [G706].

WEEDMAN -- Theiss, Gena Lee. *Christian Weedman and His Descendants, 1735-1986.* Louisville, KY, G. L. Theiss, 1986. iv, 349p., 10p. of plates. 1. Weedman family. 2. Weedman, Christian, ca. 1735-1811-Family. [G706].

WEEDMAN -- Theiss, Gena Lee. *Christian Weedman and His Descendants, 1735-1986.* Louisville, KY, G. L. Theiss, 1989. viii, 401p. 1. Weedman family. 2. Weedman, Christian, ca. 1735-1811-Family. [G706].

WEGER -- Cox, Pearl Mix. [G706]. See above: DURBIN. [G205].

WEISSENBERGER -- Conway, Jo Ann. [G707]. See above: WECKMAN. [G706].

WELLMAN -- Lane, Herbert V. *A Genealogical Record of Some Descendants of Bennett Wellman of Maryland, Virginia, West Virginia, Kentucky and North Carolina 1754-1978.* NP, 1978. 349p. [D13323].

WELLMAN -- Lane, Herbert V. *A Genealogical Record of Some Descendants of Bennett Wellman of Maryland, Virginia, West Virginia, Kentucky and North Carolina 1754-1978.* Bradenton, FL, H. V. Lane, [1978]-<1983 >. V. <1-3 >. Contents: v. 1. 1754-1978, v. 2. 1754-1980, v 3. 1754-1983. Vol. 2-<3 > called

"Supplementary Edition", Have Imprint: Decorah, Iowa, Anundsen Publising. Co. [C742; VV].

WELLS -- Henderson, Alvena Wells. *Wells Ancestors and Descendants.* Eubank, KY, A. W. Henderson, 1986. iv, 114p. 1. Wells family. 2. Kentucky-Genealogy. [G709].

WELLS -- Wells, Henry H. *Descendents of Edmund Wells and Sarah Cassity.* United

States, H. H. Wells, 1988. 2 v. 1. Wells family. 2. Wells, Edmund B., 1777-1846-Family. 3. Kentucky-Genealogy. [G709].

WELLS -- Wells, Nancy. *History of the Henton, Wells, and Drane Families.* Louisville, KY, Slater Print., 1923. 16p. [X-FW].

WERT -- Kuhn, Chella W. *Christian Wert and His Descendants.* Ft. Mitchell, KY, C. Kuhn, 1975. 167 l. [DC3887].

WEST -- Calhoun, Logan E. [G710]. See above: CALHOUN. [G115].

WEST -- Giulezan, Isabel S. *Notes on Amos West (1776-1819) of Sumner County, Tenn., and Logan County, Ky.* St. Louis, MO, 1960. 28 leaves. [X-FW].

WEST -- Ikelman, Joy A. *Leonard West (1760-1842) and Descendents (sic): A History of the West Family in Sumner County, Tennessee, Simpson County, Kentucky, and Pueble County, Colorado. ... Includes Information on Couwenhoven, Dorris, Frost, Hendricks, Holloway, McMurry, Morgan, Schenck, Wyckoff.* Longmont, CO, J. H. Ikelman, 1983. 64p. 1. West family. 2. West, Lenoard, ca. 1760-1842-Family. 3. Tennessee-Genealogy. 4. Kentucky-Genealogy. 5. Coloarado-Genealogy. [G710].

WESTALL -- Prehn, Alyene Elizabeth Westall. *Journal of a Genealogist With Ancestral Wills.*

Owensboro, KY, McDowell Publications, 1980. xliii, 829p. [D13386].

WHALEY -- Foelsch, Donald H. *An Index to Levi Kelsey Cramb's Preliminary Notes on the Whaleys of Loudon County, Va.* Williamsport, PA, 1982. [VV].

WHALLEY -- Cramb, Levi Kelsey. *Preliminary Notes on the Whaleys of Loudoun County, Virginia and of Their Descendants, Who Migrated to Kentucky.* Fairbury, NB 1943. [L18414; VV].

WHALEY -- Cramb, Levi Kelsey. *Whaleys of Loudon County, Virginia and Some of Their Descendants, Who Migrated to Kentucky.* Fairbury, NB, 1947. 30p. [L18415].

WHALEY -- Cramb, Levi Kelsey. *Whaleys of Loudon County, Virginia and Some of Their Descendants, Who Migrated to Kentucky.* NP, 1990. Originally published: 1947. 39 l. [DC3900].

WHEELER -- Minnix, Myrtle, Jayne Wheeler. *Revolutionary War Soldier "James Wheeler": His Descendants of "Concord" Near Paintsville, Kentucky, Johnson County, 1735-1981.* Ashland, KY, M. J. W. Minnix, 1982. 200 leaves. [C746].

WHETSTONE -- Horlacher, Levi Jackson. *Whetstone Family of Wilkinson County, Mississippi - Bicentennial ed. -* Lexington, KY, Horlacher, 1976. 72 leaves. 1. Whetstone family. 2. United States-Genealogy. 3. Wilkinson County (Miss.)-Genealogy. [G712; D13433].

WHETSTONE -- Horlacher, Levi Jackson. *Whetstone Family of Wilkinson County, Mississippi.* Lexington, KY, Horlacher, 1979. 79 l. [C747].

WHITAKER -- Helf, Betty M. *The Descendants of John Whitaker, 1753-1833, of Harford*

County, Maryland and Harrison County, Kentucky. San Jose, CA, B.M. Helf, Wichita, KS, J. F. Schunk, 1985. ix, 98 leaves. 1. Whitaker family. 2. Whitaker, John, 1753-1833-Family. [G713].

WHITESCARVER -- Duncan, Virginia. *Whitescarver, Weisgerber, Viscarber, Visescarver.* Utica, KY, McDowell Publications, 1983, 250p. [C750].

WHITE -- Cox, Bruce K. [G713]. See above: BOGGS. [G65].

WHITE -- White, Emery H. [G714]. See above: MAXEY. [G431].

WHITENACK -- Dietrich, M. J. S. *Whitenack Family from New Jersey to Kentucky.* College Park, MD, Author, 1972. 74p. [X-FW].

WHITESIDE -- Whiteside, Don. *Whitesides Listed in the Census of Kentucky, 1790-1850 Primarily.* NP, 1967. v, 17 leaves. [S2701].

WHITLEY -- Strader, Helen Whitley and Benbow, Routh Whitley. *Our Wandering Whitleys; Descendants of Sharp R. Whitley & John Saunders Whitley of Virginia, Kentucky, Tennessee, Illinois, Missouri and Texas and Allied Families.* Clovis, NM. viii, 264 l. [S2712; VV].

WHITMER -- Whitley, Edythe. *Whitmer, Short, Sheetz, Jones, Finch, Dozier, Kincheloe, Reno, Campbell of Mehlenburg (sic) County, Kentucky.* NP, 1938. 73 l. [D13519].

WHITNEY -- Whitney, Marylou. *Cornelia Vanderbilt Whitney's Dollhouse. The Story of a Dollhouse and the People Who Lived in It.* New York, NY, Farrar, Straus and Giroux, 1975. 115, xxx p., 2 leaves of plates. 1. Maple Hill, Ky. 2. Kentucky-Biography. 3. Whitney family. 4. Dollhouse. [G716].

WILCOX -- Payne, E. S. *Our Wilcoxon Family from North Carolina to Kentucky to Indiana and*

Westward. New Albany, IN, 1970. 452p. [X-FW].

WILFORD -- Neel, Eurie Pearl Wilford. *The Wilford-Willford Family Treks in America and a Reprint of Counties of Christian and Tregg, Kentucky, Historical and Biographical, Edited by William Henry Perrin, 1884.* Nashville, TN, 1959. 2 pts. in 1 v. (Western Kentucky Pioneer Series in V. 2). [L18685].

WILKES -- Crews, Lillian Jones. *Wilkes Records - Limited 2nd ed.* Tallahassee, FL, L.J. Crews, 1986, 1984. 283p, 2 fold. leaves of plates. "Speech given by Lillian Jones Crews at Wilkes Reunion in Paducah, Kentucky, on July 12, 1986. concerning the making of her book, Wilkes records, 1216-1984" inserted. 1. Wilkes family. 2. Great Britain-Genealogy. 3. Southern States-Genealogy. [G719].

WILKES -- Williamson, Mamie. *Wilkes Family Data, Copied by William and Anne Fitzgerald.* Florence, KY, 1954. 7 leaves. [L18689].

WILLETT -- Donnelly, Sister Mary Louise. *The Willett Family of Maryland, Colonial Pewterers, Kentucky Pioneers.* Burke, VA, M. L. Donnelly, 1983. 704p. [C755; DC3954].

WILLHOITE -- Willhoite, Leona & Earl. *John Willhoite (1745-1837) with His Descendants in Kentucky and Elsewhere.* Stroudsburg, PA, The Authors, 1987. 64p. [DC3956].

WILLIAM -- Williams, Dudley C. *Harden Williams, 1793-1875, Perry County, Kentucky: Ancestors and Descendants.* Lexington, KY, D. C. Williams, 1986. 8, 159, 15 leaves. 1. William family. 2. Williams, Harden, 1793-1875-Family. 3. Kentucky-Genealogy. [G719].

WILLIAMS -- NAS. *Biographical Record of Daniel and Mary (Jackson) Williams, Early Kentucky Pioneers. Including Portraits and Biographies of Their Children: Thomas Williams, Daniel Jackson Williams, John*

Williams, Elijah Williams, Katharine (Williams) Orr, Mary (Williams) Forsythe and Their Descendants. Together with Portrait and Biography of Andrew Jackson, the Seventh President of the United States; Also Photo-Engraving of an Old William's Homestead in Woodford County, Kentucky, Where Daniel Williams, the Pioneer and an Officer in the Revolutionary War Died. Baltimore, MD, 1898. Lexington, University of Kentucky Library, 1964. 27p. [L18779].

WILLIAMS -- Hughes, Nathaniel Cheairs. *Kentucky Memories of Uncle Sam Williams.* Chatanooga, TN, Hughes, 1978. xii, 133p. [D13649].

WILLIAMS -- Kelley, Julielma M. *Biographical Record of Daniel and Mary (Jackson) Williams, Early Kentucky Pioneers... 1752-1898.* Baltimore, MD, 1898. 27p. FW copy lacks p. 28-29. [X-FW/SU].

WILLIAMS -- McMurry, Rhuy K. *One Branch of our Williams Family of Maryland and Kentucky.* NP, 1974. 205p. [NG103].

WILLIAMS -- Roper, Mary Louise Gaw. [G720]. See above: GAW. [G253].

WILLIAMS -- Savage, Bertha Williams. *We Are The Williams.* Wurtland, KY, Savage, 1978. 69p. [C756; D13661].

WILLIAMS -- Stinson, Era W. [G721]. See above: TAYLOR. [G652].

WILLIAMS -- Williams, Charles Lee. *A Williams Genealogy.* Tulsa, OK, C.L. Williams, 1985. 19, 20 leaves. Cover Title: William & Mary Williams & their descendants of early Gallatin & Carroll County, Kentucky from the 1790's. 1. Williams family. 2. Kentucky-Genealogy. [G721].

WILLIAMS -- Williams, Dudley C. *Morris Williams, 1791/1873, Harrison County,*

Kentucky: Ancestors and Descendants. Lexington, KY, D. C. Williams, 1985. 116 leaves. 1. Williams family. 2. Williams, Morris, 1791-1873-Family. 3. Harrison County (Ky.)-Genealogy. [G721].

WILLIAMS -- Williams, Samuel. *Kentucky Memories of Uncle Sam Williams.* Chattanooga, TN, 1978. 133p. [NG103].

WILLIAMSON -- Alley, Joseph W. *Alden Williamson Genealogy; A Genealogical Record of Alden Williamson's Family in Pike, Martin, Floyd, Johnson, Lawrence and Boyd Counties in Kentucky and Mingo, Wayne, Logan, Lincoln, Cabell and Wyoming Counties in West Virginia.* Prichard, WV, 1962. 254p. [X-FW].

WILSON -- Pavlick, Lynde Louise McElroy. *The Wilson Family of Montgomery County, Illinois, Indiana and Kentucky.* Worcester MA, Pavlick, 1979. 165p. [C758].

WILSON -- Wilson, Jess D. *When They Hanged the Fiddler and Other Stories from "It Happened Here". Including Some Unpublished Works by the Author.* Berea, KY, Kentucke (sic) Imprints, 1978. iv, 260p. [C759].

WILSON -- Wilson, Jess D. *The Sugar Pond and Fritter Tree.* Berea, KY, Kentucke (sic) Imprints, 1981. ii, 215p. 1. Kentucky-Social life and customs. 2. Kentucky-biography. 3. Wilson family. 4. Wilson, Jess D. [G724; C759].

WILSON -- Wilson, William Surber. *Family Tree.* Ingle, KY, 1982. 1 v. (various pagings). [C759].

WITHERSPOON -- Witherspoon, Martinette Viley. *My Ancestors; A Brief Account of the Ancestry of Lister Witherspoon and His Wife, Martinette Viley of Woodford County, Kentucky.* Washington, DC, 1922. 303, 13p. Allied Families: Martin Rhodes-Thomas, Douglas, Heale, Smith of "Purton", and others. [L18955].

WITT -- Cox, Pearl Mix. [G730]. See above: DURBIN. [G205].

WOOD -- NAS. *Descendants of Josiah Wood Through His Son David Wood, Albermarle County, Virginia.* Hopkinsville, KY, 1947. 6p. [L19040].

WOOD -- Peden, Henry C. *The William Wood and Related Families of Albermarle County, Virginia and Barren County, Kentucky in the 1800's.* Bel Air, VA, Henry C. Peden, 1984. 45 leaves. [DC4012; VV].

WOOD -- Wood, Edith L. *The Wood and Allied Families.* Middletown, KY, 1973. NY has 2 vols. FW has 3 vols. [X-FW;NY].

WOOD -- Wood, William L. *Samuel Wood: His Seven Sons and Their Descendants: Virginia to North Carolina, Tennessee, Kentucky, Illinois, and Beyond, 1755-1988.* Strafford, MO, W. L. Wood, 1988. xii, 320, 134p. 1. Wood family. 2. Wood, Samuel, 1737-ca.1800-Family. [G734].

WOOD -- Woods, Rev. Neander M. *The Woods - McAfee Memorial, Containing an Account of John Woods and James McAfee of Ireland and Their Descendants in America... in Which , Besides Considerable New Material Bearing on Virginia and Kentucky History Will Be Found Mention of the Families of Adams, Alexander, Behre, Bennett, etc... Also Some Hitherto Unpublished Documents Which Constitute a Valuable Contribution to the Pioneer History of Virginia and Kentucky.* Louisville, KY, Courier-Journal, 1905. 503p. [D13910].

WOOLFOLK -- Davis, W. F. *Genealogy of the Male Line of the Ancestors of Sowyel Woolfolk, Born in Virginia, 1774, Died in Woodford County, Ky., 1830.* Kansas City, MO, 1948. 5, 11p. [X-FW; VV].

WOODRING -- Basham, Kay Joyce Yates. *The Woodring- Richardson Family of Hardin County, Kentucky.* Louisville, KY, K. J. Y. Basham, 1984. 19 leaves. [C766].

WOODSON -- Koerner, Patsy Ann (Hammons). *Wade Netherland Woodson, I (Wade N.; W. N.) and Reason Warfield, I.* Louisville, KY, Knox County Genealogical Society, 1982. 34 leaves. [C766].

WORSLEY -- Woosley, Laura and Arthur Lee McLaughlin. *The Woosley Family History.* Ownesboro, KY, McDowell Publications, 1979, iii, 24 leaves. [C768].

WORSLEY -- Woosley, Laura and Arthur Lee McLaughlin. *The Woosley Family History.*

Ownesboro, KY, McDowell Publications, 1981, iii, 159 leaves. [C768].

WRIGHT -- Cain, Marilynn Wright Duffner. [G736]. See above: BOEDECKER. [G64].

WRIGHT -- Ritchie, Ann Reed. *Supplement, Corrections and Additions to Major Francis Wright and Ann Washington, with Allied Families.* Ownesboro, KY, McDowell Publications, 1979. 105p. [C770.

WRIGHT -- Stoops, Mary De Forest Waldrop. *Descendants of William Wright and Amos Wright of North Carolina, Kentucky and Indiana.* NP, 1959. 72, 32 l. [D13978].

WYNN -- Simpson, George Brown. *From Tidewater to Tradewater: Biography of Rev. William Watkins Wynns.* Sturgis, KY, M & M Printing, 1979. 10, 113p., 2 leaves of plates. 1. Wynns, William Watkins, 1839-1900. 2. Presbyterian Church-Clergy-Biography. 3. Clergy-United States-Biography. 4. Wynn family. [G738].

WYNN -- Winn, James French. *Winn Memoirs; Jesse Durrett Winn, His Family and Descendants.* Cynthiana, KY, The Hobson Press, 1942. 2, vii-ix, 49p. [L19206].

XY

YATES -- Basham, Kay Joyce Yates. *The Yates Family of Hardin County, Kentucky.* Louisville, KY, K. J. Y. Basham, 1984. 9, 55 l. [C772].

YATES -- Cox, Opal London. [G739]. See above: BEWLEY. [G54]

YODER -- Yoder, Charles M. *Brief Record of Four Pioneer Families of St. Joseph County, Indiana: Yoder, Webster, Swaim , Hunt.* Louisville, KY, J. M. Yoder, 1958. 54p. 3 leaves. [X-FW].

YOUNG -- Tipton, Whitney Hord. *The Young Family.* Mt. Sterling, KY, Tipton, 1953. 1 v. unpaged. D gives ca.200p. [L19270; D14062].

YOUNG -- Wooten, Jessamine Young. *John Young, Kentucky Pioneer, and His Kin.* Huntsville, AL, Wooten, 1972. 414p. [D14064].

YOUNG -- Young, Asher Leon. *Washington Young of Wayne County, Kentucky, and His Descendants.* Nashville, TN, Young, 1975. 217p. 1. Young family. 2. United States-Genealogy. 3. Wayne County (Ky.)-Genealogy. [G741; X-FW/NY].

Z

ZIEGENFUSS -- Zickefoose, Larry C. *From Zigenfuss to Zickefoose, 1739-1900.* Baltimore, MD, Gateway Press, Covington, KY, L. C. Zickefoose, 1990. x, 163p., 5 p. of plates. 1. Ziegenfuss family. 2. West Virginia-Genealogy. [G743].

ZIMMERMAN -- Moore, Willa M.D. *Records of Frederick Zimmerman, Esq., Jessamine Co., Kentucky.* NP, 1960. 60 leaves in various foliations. [D14100].

ZIMMERMAN -- Lloyd, Emma Rouse. *Zimmerman Family of Pennsylvania and Kentucky.* NP, n.d., pages not shown. (Available for Consultation at the Lloyd Library, 309 West Court St., Cincinnati, OH.) [L19304].

ZOLLICOFFER -- Myers, Raymond E. *The Zollie Tree.* Louisville, KY, Filson Club Press, 1964. xiii, 200p. [D14107].

BIBLIOGRAPHIC SOURCES

GRUNDSET, Eric B. & Bebe, Metz. Library Catalog, Volume Three Centennial Supplement: Acquisitions 1985-1991. Washington, DC, NATIONAL SOCIETY of the DAUGHTERS of the AMERICAN REVOLUTION, 1992.

KAMINKOW, Marion J. Genealogies In The Library of Congress. Baltimore, 1972. 2. v. A-J and L-Z.

KAMINKOW, Marion J. Genealogies In The Library of Congress, Supplement 1972 - 1976. Baltimore: Magna Carta Book Company, 1976.

KAMINKOW, Marion J. Genealogies In The Library of Congress, Second Supplement 1976 - 1986. Baltimore: Magna Carta Book Company, 1987.

KAMINKOW, Marion J. A Complement To Genealogies In The Library of Congress. Baltimore: Magna Carta Book Company, 1981.

LIB. OF CONGRESS STAFF Genealogies Cataloged in the Library of Congress Since 1986. Washington, DC, Cataloging Distribution Service, Library of Congress, 1991.

NGS LIBRARY STAFF National Genealogical Society, Library Book List, 5th Edition. Arlington, Virginia, National Genealogical Society. 1988.

NGS LIBRARY STAFF National Genealogical Society, Library Book List, 5th Edition Supplement. Arlington, Virginia, National Genealogical Society. 1989.

MICHAELS, Carolyn Leopold and Kathryn S. Scott. Library Catalog, Volume One, Second Revised Edition, Family Histories and Genealogies. Washington, DC, National Society of the Daughters of the American Revolution, 1983.

MICHAELS, Carolyn Leopold and Kathryn S. Scott. Library Catalog, Volume One - Supplement - Family Histories and Genealogies. Washington, DC, National Society of the Daughters of the American Revolution, 1984.

VIRDIN, Donald O. Virginia Genealogies and Family Histories. Bowie, Maryland, Heritage Books, Inc., 1990.

VIRDIN, Donald O. Pennsylvania Genealogies and Family Histories. Bowie, Maryland, Heritage Books, Inc., 1992.

This cross-reference table lists family names given in titles and accompanying descriptive statements recorded in this bibliography.